IMAGES
of America

HUNTSVILLE

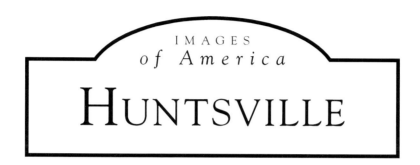

IMAGES
of America

HUNTSVILLE

John F. Kvach, Charity Ethridge,
Michelle Hopkins, and Susanna Leberman

ARCADIA
PUBLISHING

Published by Arcadia Publishing
Charleston, South Carolina

Printed in the United States of America

Library of Congress Control Number: 2012951110

For all general information, please contact Arcadia Publishing:
Telephone 843-853-2070
Fax 843-853-0044
E-mail sales@arcadiapublishing.com
For customer service and orders:
Toll-Free 1-888-313-2665

Visit us on the Internet at www.arcadiapublishing.com

*To those people who have helped make Huntsville's
history a rich one, whether or not they knew it at the
time, and to those who are no longer with us.*

CONTENTS

ACKNOWLEDGMENTS

We would like to acknowledge the support of the Huntsville–Madison County Public Library and the University of Alabama in Huntsville's Public History Program. Both of these institutions have given time and talent to make this book possible. Specifically, it is important to highlight the service of Elisabeth Spalding, John O'Brien, Nancy Rohr, Brian Hogan, Jacqueline Proctor Reeves, Lance George, Donna Dunham, and Ranee Pruitt.

We would also like to acknowledge the staff of the library's Heritage Room: Richard White, Thomas Hutchens, and Dorcus Raunich, as well as Donna Barlow, the archivist of the Huntsville–Madison County Records Center, and Diane Long, the archivist of Madison County's tax assessor office. Without their help and encouragement, this book would have been difficult to undertake and impossible to finish. Their help along the way made all of the difference.

These photographs do not tell the complete story of Huntsville, but we hope they show a different side of the city's history. All images appear courtesy of the Huntsville–Madison County Public Library. The authors of this book have generously donated all their profits to the University of Alabama in Huntsville's Public History Program.

INTRODUCTION

A pictorial history of Huntsville is much more than a collection of old black-and-white photographs of people, places, and buildings. The photographs in this book represent the very definition of history: change over time. Life in Huntsville has changed because the world around it has changed since the city's founding in the early 1800s. Cotton planters, merchants, and entrepreneurs moved into northern Alabama in search of new opportunities created by rich soil, slave labor, and hard work. Busy residents quickly made Huntsville an economic and social hub for southerners living on the cotton frontier. Large plantations, busy railroads, and bustling factories defied the stereotypical visions of a languid "Old South" town. Huntsville emerged as a prominent city long before deceptive "New South" boosters promoted their false dreams of a more modern post–Civil War South.

The Civil War brought heartache and pain for some city residents and freedom for others. As an occupied city during the war, Huntsville failed to serve the South's needs. But the city quickly reemerged as the center of cotton production for much of northern Alabama. Like many Southern towns and cities after the Civil War, the city experienced difficult times associated with slave emancipation, racial violence, political upheaval, and an overreliance on cotton. By World War II, however, Huntsville had once again reinvented itself, as the federal government and private contractors and corporations made the city a center of military and space technology. Instead of becoming just another sleepy Southern hamlet, Huntsville emerged as the technological axis for a nation interested in space flight. The rapid development of NASA's Marshall Space Center and Redstone Arsenal added diversity of thought and people into an already diverse city.

New development often obscures past achievements, and many residents do not understand the long history of Huntsville. This book attempts to highlight some of the past successes and failures through the use of photographs, not because they stand for steady progress for a select group of people, but because photographs represent the broader forces of familiarity and community. Some of these photographs are recognizable, while others will challenge readers to think of Huntsville before it became "Rocket City, USA."

Huntsville has changed a great deal over time, and many of these photographs reflect the subtle and drastic changes that mark a community's history. In the early 1800s, the average resident would have walked or ridden a horse around the city. By the end of that century, that same resident would have been able to walk on new sidewalks, ride a bike on paved roads, take a trolley, or drive a car. Candles gave way to electricity, and city boundaries yielded to bedroom communities that allowed people to work in Huntsville and live in the suburbs. Ultimately, the convenience of cars and modern highways doomed Huntsville's downtown. Compared to past generations, few people today live, work, or play in downtown Huntsville. This is changing, however, as city leaders and private individuals push to recreate a vibrant downtown.

Historical photographs provide clues for understanding how downtown Huntsville once looked. It is important to remember that these photographs only capture a moment of time and do not represent the complete narrative of past memories. Historians rely on these primary sources because they often offer the best opportunity to recreate a more accurate portrayal of the past. Think about the images and what it must have been like before and after the photograph was taken. Smiling faces may have been hiding deeper pain created by economic panic, racial discrimination, gender bias, or just a bad day. Instead of just looking at what is in these photographs, take time to think about what is missing from them. Where are the photographs of the Native Americans who lived on the land before John Hunt arrived in 1805? Why are there no photographs of any one of the thousands of slaves who lived and worked in Huntsville? Why did local photographers never stray into the darker alleys of Huntsville to show what life looked like for those less fortunate? These are the types of questions that will enhance the interpretation of these photographs. Remember that photographers have the power to shape what is seen and not seen. For every group of smiling men in bowler hats, there was likely a corresponding group of women and children not deemed worthy of their own photograph. Look beyond the clothes, landscapes, and buildings; think about the history and ask why. Each photograph holds clues to the past—find them.

Locals are currently adding another chapter to Huntsville's history, but, like most of the subjects in these photographs, they are not thinking about their lives in a historical context. The clothes we wear today, the cars we drive, and the building styles we prefer are being recorded by photographers looking to capture moments in time. In 100 years, future residents of Huntsville will laugh at current hairstyles, admire current contributions to the city, and wonder about shortsightedness. This is a natural part of the historical process. Local history provides a unique perspective because it allows historians to see what life was really like for the average American. Local history emphasizes the familiar: the people in these photographs woke up, went to work, raised families, had fun, felt pain, and lived life. They felt as strongly about their past and future as we do now. They built monuments to fallen soldiers, preserved old buildings, and maintained archives so future generations would understand the commitment and sacrifice of those who helped build Huntsville. However, do not forget about the silent voices that also helped create a sense of community and contributed to the history in Huntsville.

One

BUILDING HUNTSVILLE

Huntsville owed much of its early growth to the production of cotton and the expansion of the railroad system. Wealthy planters moved here to cultivate and sell cotton. As cotton production increased around Huntsville, the city grew correspondingly to fit the needs of its citizens. In 1850, it was announced that the Memphis & Charleston Railroad would be moving to Huntsville. The railroad had a great impact on the city during the Civil War. Many new businesses popped up around the square, including hotels, attorney's offices, doctor's offices, merchant shops, and beautiful churches. All of this reflected the success of the city.

Many in Huntsville did not support the decision to secede from the Union in 1861. The city, however, provided many soldiers to the Confederacy—and even some to the Union. In 1862, Union troops seized Huntsville in efforts to cut rail communication throughout the Confederacy. The troops retreated, but returned again in 1863, occupying Huntsville for the duration of the war. While the Union troops were stationed in Huntsville, they burned many homes and buildings, but most of the city was left unharmed because it housed the troops and their camps.

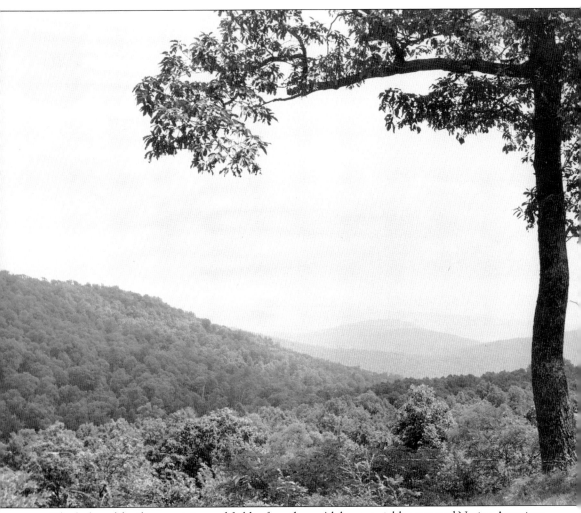

The lush and fertile mountains and fields of northern Alabama quickly attracted Native American, Spanish, English, and American settlers over time. Each group envisioned using the region's natural resources differently, making what is now Huntsville a contested area by the early 1800s. After the Spanish evacuated the Mississippi Territory in 1797, the United States and the state of Georgia claimed what is now Madison County, Alabama. By 1802, Georgia had relinquished its claim, but that did not stop thousands of settlers from moving into northern Alabama. In 1806, the US government purchased a triangle of land wedged between the Tennessee border and the Tennessee River. In 1809, this spit of land became known as Madison County, and thousands of new settlers began to look for productive land in the area that is now Huntsville.

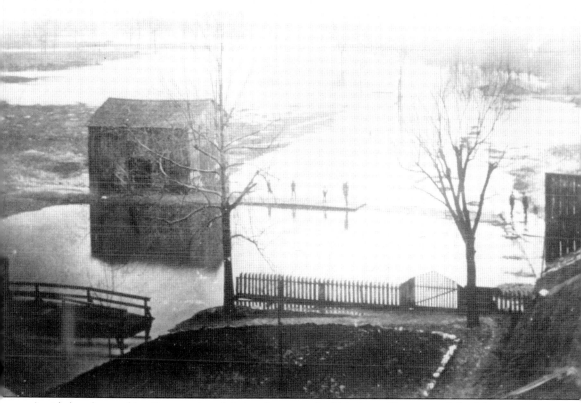

Amid the chaos of jostling empires fighting for control of Madison County and the Mississippi Territory, John Hunt left his home in Franklin County, Tennessee, and traveled south on the Winchester Road in search of a suitable homestead and rich farmland. During his trip, he stopped and stayed with Isaac Criner, who lived along the Flint River near what is now New Market, Alabama. Eventually, Hunt ventured 15 miles south and settled along a natural spring in what is now downtown Huntsville. Early Huntsville resident Anne Royall described Hunt as: "Standing 5 feet 10 inches in height, his 180 pounds were a mass of flexible steel." Although Hunt initially claimed the land, speculators and planters from Georgia quickly moved in and gained control of it. LeRoy Pope outbid other buyers at a land auction and began the process that transformed the cotton frontier into a bustling town and commercial hub for the early settlers of northern Alabama. This photograph shows Hunt's water source, now known as Big Spring, during a heavy spring rain in the early 1900s.

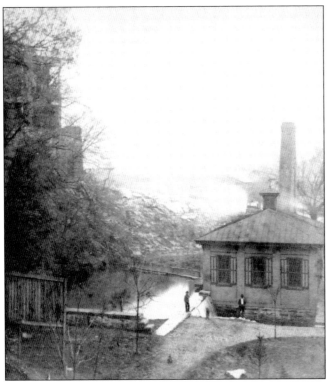

The importance of fresh water made Big Spring an essential element in Huntsville's steady growth in the 1800s. Fearful of human and animal waste and manmade pollution, early city leaders passed an ordinance to guarantee this water source. This photograph shows Big Spring and a pump house that the city built in 1860. Part of the First National Bank can be seen at top left.

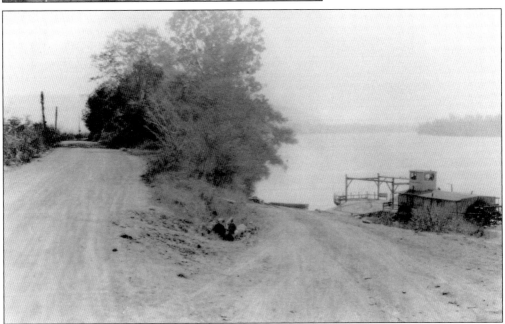

The nearby Tennessee River served as an important transportation link for early settlers in Huntsville. In 1810, James Ditto started a ferry and shipyard near what is now the Whitesburg Bridge. During the Creek War of 1813–1814, Davy Crockett recalled marching with Andrew Jackson: "We went on and crossed the Tennessee River at a place called Ditto's landing; and then traveled about seven miles further [to Huntsville]."

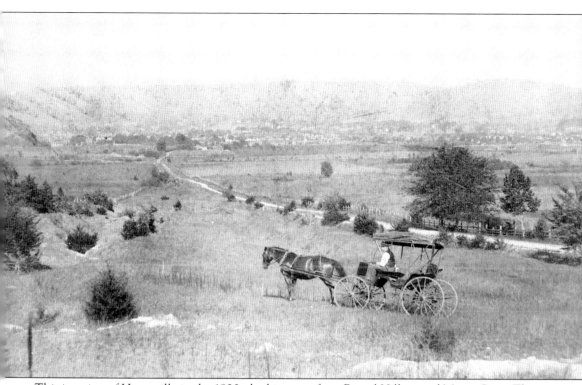

This is a view of Huntsville in the 1800s, looking east from Russel Hill toward Monte Sano. The growing city of Huntsville lies at the base of the mountain that looms in the distance. Albert Russel, an early resident of Huntsville and a Revolutionary War veteran, settled on this prominent hill overlooking the growing town after John Hunt had settled in the area. In 1859, Alexander Erskine, a direct descendant of Albert Russel, put his 600-acre estate up for sale after the longtime resident had died. This photograph provides a useful perspective of modern Huntsville's growth and the blight of urban sprawl. Today, the same view includes homes, apartments, businesses, gas stations, and obtrusive expanses of concrete and raised highway. Although early residents referred to the meandering farm lane in the middle of the photograph as Athens Pike, modern residents of Huntsville know it as Holmes Avenue.

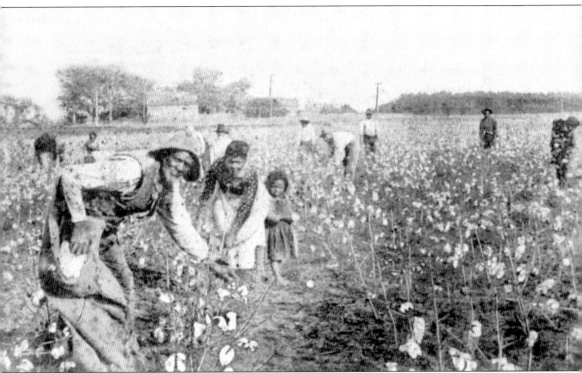

The earliest settlers of Huntsville and Madison County relied heavily on the cultivation and sale of cotton, and on slaves. Early travel writer Anne Royall visited Madison County in 1818 and described Huntsville and its surrounding countryside as being "rich and beautiful as you can imagine; and the appearance of wealth would baffle belief . . . the cotton fields are astonishingly large. Four or five hundred acres in a field without parallel, although the land is level you cannot see the end of the fields either way." Early settlers grabbed as much land as they could from Native Americans and began to plant cotton. Cotton's popularity had increased after Eli Whitney's invention of the cotton gin in 1793. This photograph highlights the backbreaking work that most slaves faced while working in the early cotton fields outside of Huntsville. Much of the wealth and prosperity of the city came from slave labor.

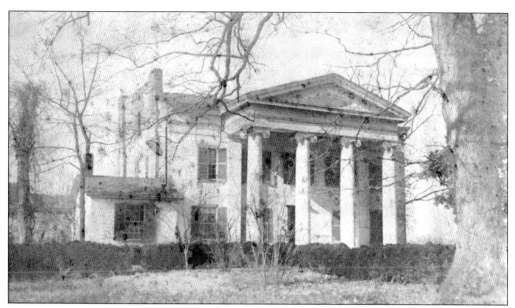

Located near the present-day Huntsville Hospital, Grove Plantation served as a reminder of the vast wealth cotton created in the region. This grand plantation house was built in the early 1820s and became the center for social activity among Huntsville's elite planter class. Although many modern Americans think of large plantations and slaves as common elements of the "Old South," in reality, only a small minority of Southerners could afford to live on large plantations.

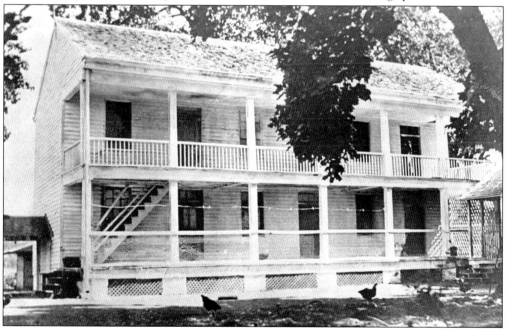

A territorial census reported that Madison County's population had swelled to 14,200 residents and 4,200 slaves by 1816. The number of slaves would continue to increase as planters and farmers developed more land for cotton cultivation. This photograph shows slave quarters on Quietdale Plantation. At the peak of its pre–Civil War existence, Quietdale housed more than 100 slaves in buildings such as this one.

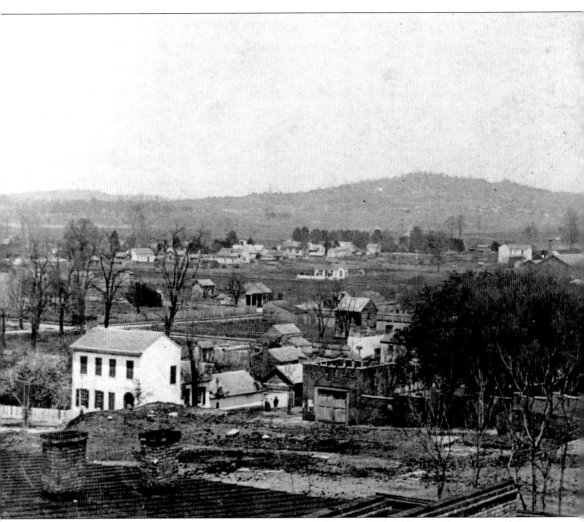

This photograph was taken from the present site of the YMCA building at the corner of Greene Street and Randolph Avenue. City homes speckled the landscape around Big Spring and along Clinton, Randolph, and Eustis Avenues. By 1861, the city had grown to become a regional commercial center and transportation hub. Robert Caldwell, a Union soldier in the Civil War, noted, "Huntsville has the reputation of being the finest city in Alabama. The streets are well shaded, there are numerous fine residences in and around town, some of the finest gardens and yards I ever saw. The houses are literally imbedded in trees and flowers, and such roses!!! I thought I had seen some roses in our front yard at home, but that is as nothing compared with some of the yards in this city, although I would give more to see our pleasant front yard, than to own all the flowers in the South." Caldwell was wounded at the Battle of Stones River in Murfreesboro, Tennessee, and died in a military hospital in February 1863.

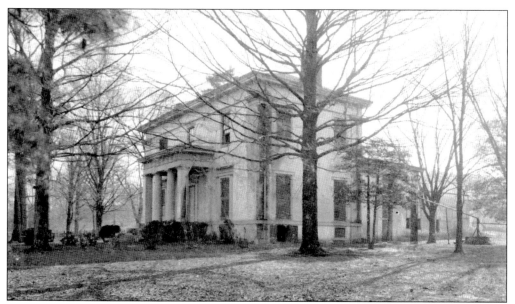

George Steele, considered by many to be one of Huntsville's greatest architects, arrived in the city in 1818 and built the beautiful home above, Oak Place, on Maysville Road. Steele also designed the Huntsville Female Seminary, Huntsville Female College, and the Planters' and Merchants' Bank, along the west side of Courthouse Square. Steele became famous for his Greek Revival style of architecture. He continued to design buildings and homes for wealthy Huntsville residents until his death on October 21, 1855. Steele was buried in Maple Hill Cemetery but was later moved to Birmingham to be buried next to his son. Below, Theodopolos Lacey, a teller at the Planters' and Merchants' Bank in the 1800s, stands on the front steps of the bank. Lacey lived in an apartment on the top floor of the building.

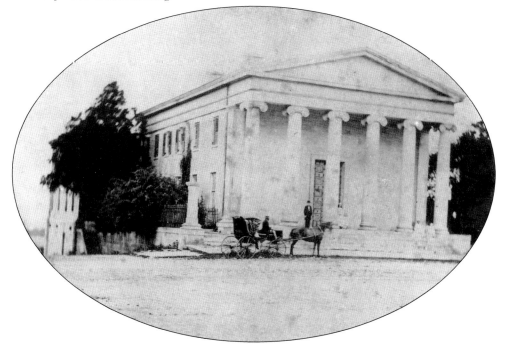

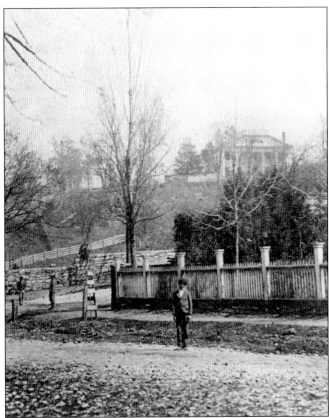

This is a view of the Pope home, Poplar Grove, which was built in 1815 on Patton Hill, a prominent hill near downtown Huntsville. Although Pope died in June 1844, the name of the house remained the same until Dr. Charles H. Patton, the president of a local factory, purchased the property. Patton Hill was the headquarters for Union troops during their occupation of Huntsville in the Civil War.

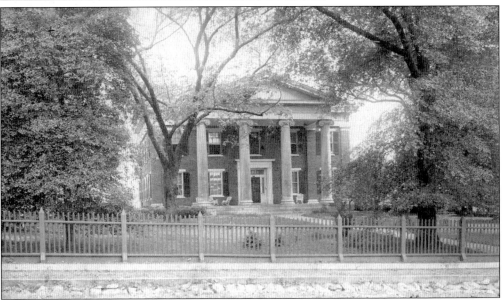

Thomas Bibb built this mansion for his daughter Adeline in 1836. Unfortunately for Adeline, her husband, James Bradley, lost the home to debtors in 1844. Family legend says that Adeline learned of her loss when the new owner's gardener showed up to plant bulbs in the garden. In 1927, descendants of the Bibb family repurchased the home, and it remains in their possession today.

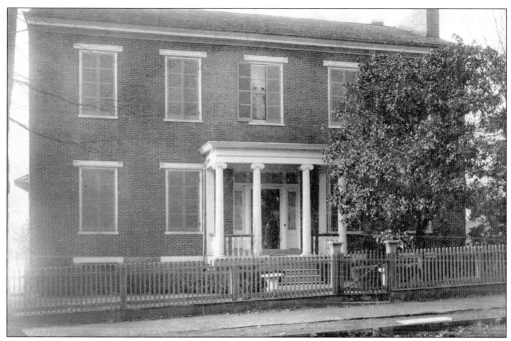

The Clarke-Powell Home, at 518 Adams Street, has a unique history in Huntsville's early development. Built in 1835 for Susan Clarke, the house was owned by women from 1835 to 1924, with the exception of John F. Fackler, who owned the home from 1859 to 1871. After Fackler's death in 1871, his daughter Sarah Fackler Pynchon inherited the home.

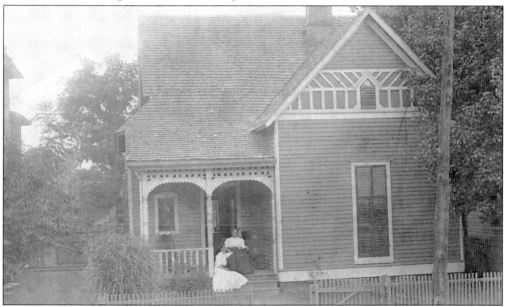

As Huntsville developed into a commercial and agricultural hub for much of northern Alabama, new businesses and homes sprung up around the city's downtown area. Here, Mrs. C.S. Vann sits in her rocking chair on the front porch with her daughter Laura Vann. The Vann family owned a jewelry and watch-repair business on Washington Street across from Dunnavant's storefront. The Vann house is located at 421 Clinton Avenue.

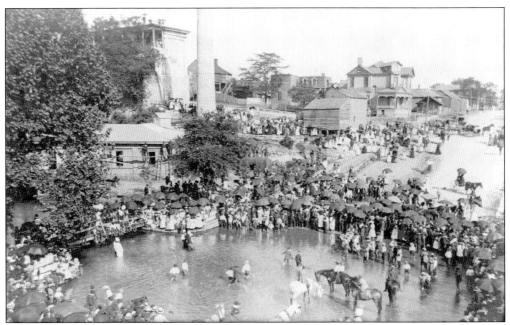

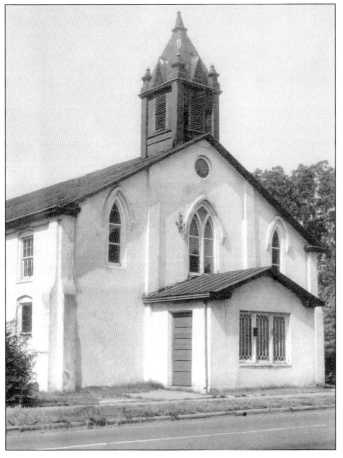

Rich African American traditions developed in Huntsville in the 1800s. On May 18, 1893, a photographer captured Rev. William H. Gaston officiating a baptism at Big Spring (above). The Huntsville African Baptist Church was organized in 1820 after the slaves of Huntsville came together to worship in the slave cemetery known as Old Georgia Graveyard. William Harris served as the first pastor of the church. This congregation is known today as St. Bartley Primitive Baptist Church, named after Rev. Bartley Harris. After the original church building was burned by Union troops during the Civil War, another church was rebuilt with money from the government in 1872. The new structure (left) featured Gothic windows with ornamental glass and grey stucco.

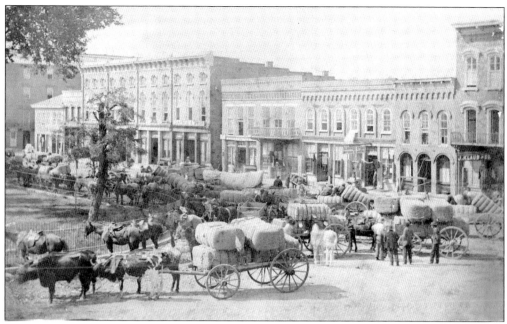

The red clay of northern Alabama produced high-quality cotton and made Madison County a top producer of cotton after the Civil War. This photograph was taken in 1871 and shows how important the city's downtown square was for commercial cotton traders and farmers, or for just catching up with friends. The grassy area on the left is where the current courthouse stands.

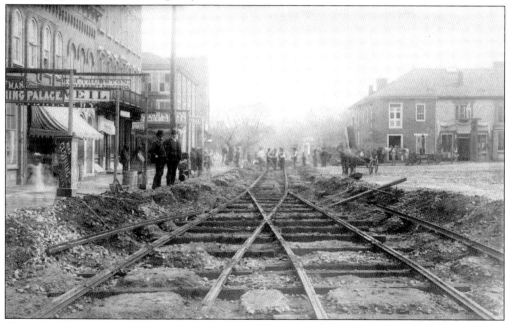

Urban growth meant new means of transportation for the excited residents of downtown Huntsville. Here, workers lay tracks for streetcars in 1888. In the background, people are busy working on the line while spectators watch the work being done. The development of a vibrant downtown commercial sector can also be seen in the shop signs in the distance, which include advertisements for grocery stores, millinery goods, and clothing shops.

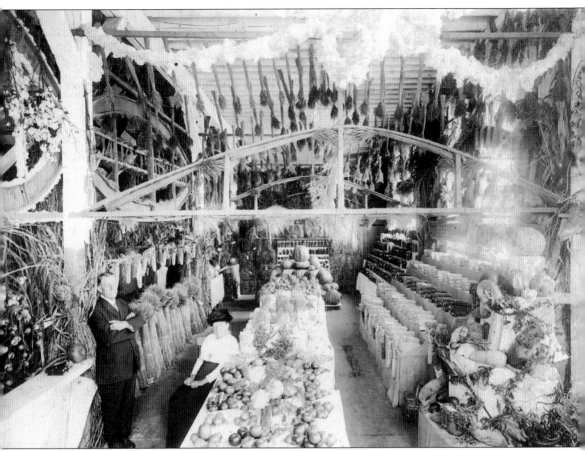

Headlines in the centennial edition of the *Huntsville Mercury* on July 23, 1916, read, "Madison County's Remarkable Productiveness Makes It The Ideal Location For Farmers: Diversification Is The Only Salvation Of Southern Farmers." The article featured this photograph of Madison County's prize-winning exhibit at the state fair in Birmingham in 1915. One of the judges remarked, "You have everything that grows in the ground." The superintendent of the exhibit, George I. Motz, wrote a detailed essay about his success in which he presented arguments for progress and the possibilities of achieving diversification. His first argument was the imperative need to "dethrone King Cotton." He believed farming was a science and argued that one of the reasons Madison County won nearly every first prize in expositions in Georgia, Alabama, and Mississippi was because farmers communicated their experiments and "interchange of thought." According to Motz, "A fair is supposed to secure the best product grown in any section of the country." He explained that Madison County has 18 soil types, and through scientific and practical agriculture, citizens can shout together "Eureka."

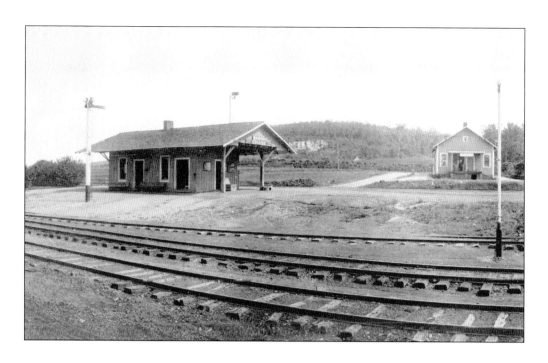

Henry B. Chase was born on June 13, 1870, in Livermore, Maine, and arrived in Huntsville when he was 19. From 1889 to 1906, he worked with his brothers to develop a nursery business with capital provided by his family. His business eventually became Chase Nursery in 1906. In the 1971 *Huntsville Historical Review*, Dr. Frances Roberts wrote that the brothers chose the 1,000-acre plot of land "because of its accessibility to railroad lines and the beautiful, rich loamy soil." The Chase Nursery depot is above, and the residences at the nursery are below. Henry Chase was a pioneer in the wholesale nursery business and served as the mayor of Huntsville from 1918 to 1920.

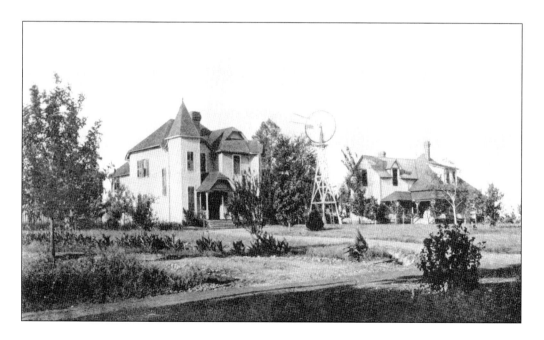

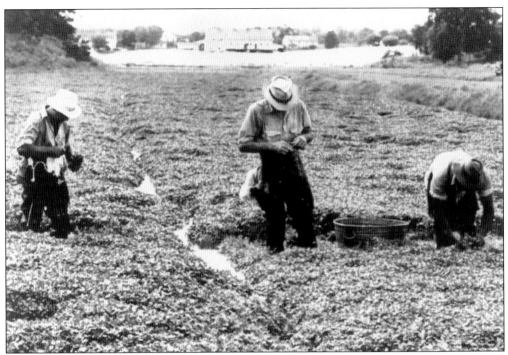

Frank Dennis moved from New Jersey to Huntsville when demand for watercress increased among American consumers in the late 1800s. Dennis needed more land and a better climate to raise the leafy vegetable for wealthy northern restaurateurs and hotel owners. An early Dennis watercress brochure noted that he "bought land in Huntsville, Alabama, and turned the springs into channels and the meadows into ponds, and planted the ponds to water cress." The brochure described how farm laborers had to wear "high hip-length boots, carry stout even lengths of twine at their belts for tying the bunches and with their sharp knives move up the pond . . . cutting in rhythmical strokes; a length of twine, a few deft twists of the wrist and a flip over the shoulder to the men carrying tubs."

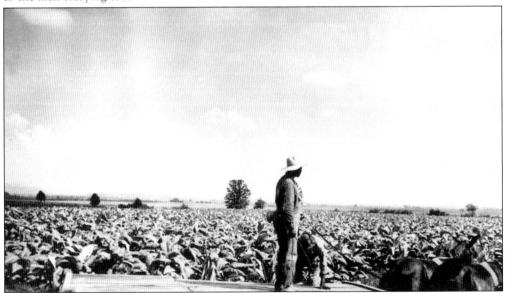

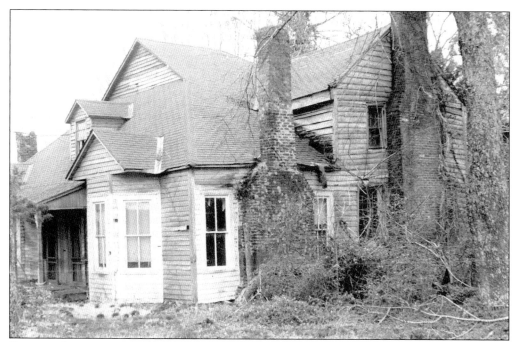

Crops such as cotton and watercress made the farmland around Huntsville more valuable, and early settlers began to improve their homesteads as profits increased over time. Dr. James Manning moved to Madison County in 1809. A year later, he had this two-story cabin built near Meridianville. He later sold the home and moved to Huntsville.

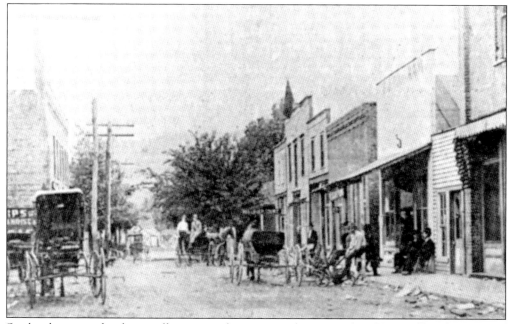

Settlers began to develop small towns in the countryside surrounding Huntsville. This scene of busy downtown Gurley is indicative of the importance of town development around Madison County in the 1800s. Agricultural goods flowed from nearby fields to these small towns before moving to Huntsville and then on to larger markets.

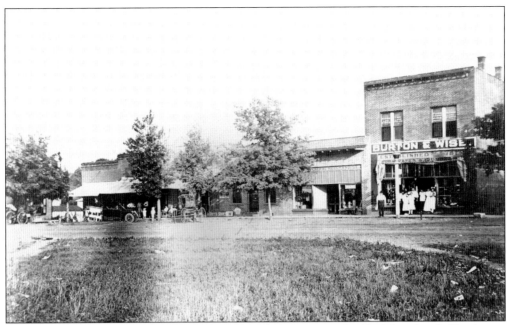

The town of Madison was originally known as Madison Station after the Memphis & Charleston Railroad extended railroad track to the area in 1856. Note that automobiles and wagons still share the roadway in this early 1900s photograph. Proud residents and customers stand in front of the Burton & Wise drugstore at a time before electric lines transformed the landscape.

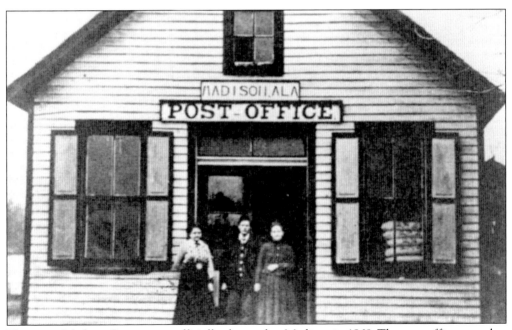

The name Madison Station was officially changed to Madison in 1869. The post office served as a natural social center for residents who were picking up and sending their mail. Although this building no longer exists, the downtown area is still the center of Madison and was placed on the National Register of Historic Places in 2006.

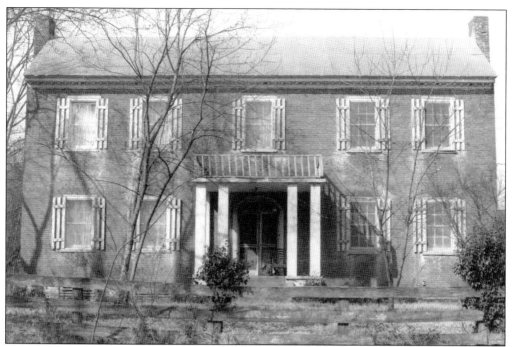

Isaac and Joseph Criner settled in northeastern Madison County in the early 1800s, and by 1806, enough people had moved into the area to form the town of New Market. Located just outside of Huntsville, New Market became a prosperous farming community. In 1830, Joseph Laughinghouse built this house on Bell Factory Road near New Market.

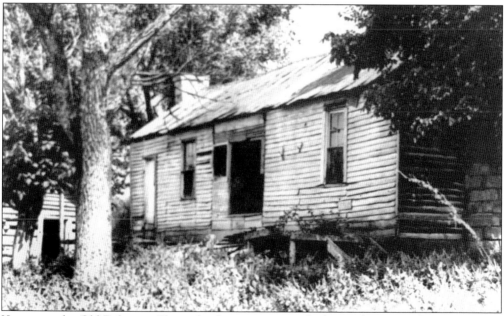

Known as the Old Robinson Place, this house was typical of many homes in the New Market area in the 1800s. Much of the lumber used to build these houses came from local forests and was cut by nearby lumber mills and farmers looking to make extra money. Modern siding and new windows now cover up the history of many early homes.

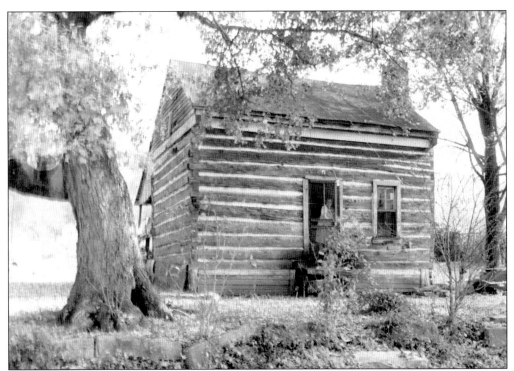

Located on Upper Mountain Fork Road in New Market, the Snyder-Fanning log house was built by Crusun Snyder in 1883. Altie Snyder Fanning, who lived in the home for more than 50 years, stands in the doorway. She later told the *Huntsville Times*, "I guess I have gone from quilting bees to electric blankets, and watched mud-holes turned into paved roads right in front of my door."

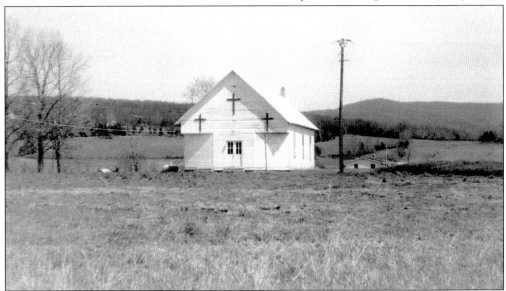

In many small rural communities such as Gurley, Madison, and New Market, rural churches became important religious and social centers for isolated farmers. In this photograph of Hickory Grove Church, on Upper Hurricane Road near New Market, the undeveloped fields and mountains of Madison County have yet to be consumed by Huntsville's urban sprawl.

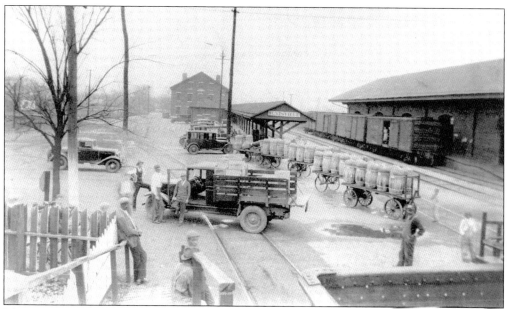

The arrival of railroads in the 1850s helped stimulate Huntsville's economy and made it an important railroad hub for the rest of the century. These early 1900s photographs highlight the city's busy railroad depot, roundhouse, and machine shops. During the Civil War, the Union and the Confederacy fought to gain control of Huntsville. On April 11, 1862, local diarist Mary Jane Chadick wrote, "General Mitchell's division took possession of Huntsville. There was no opposition there being only a few wounded and sick Confederate soldiers in the town. They entered at daybreak, first taking possession of the railroad and some 15 engines. The southern train was just coming in, having aboard 159 Confederate soldiers, some wounded. The train endeavored to make its escape, but was fired into by 2 cannons. All on board were taken prisoner, the well were confined to the Depot, the wounded left on the cars."

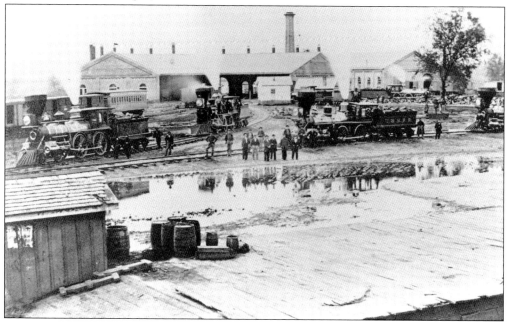

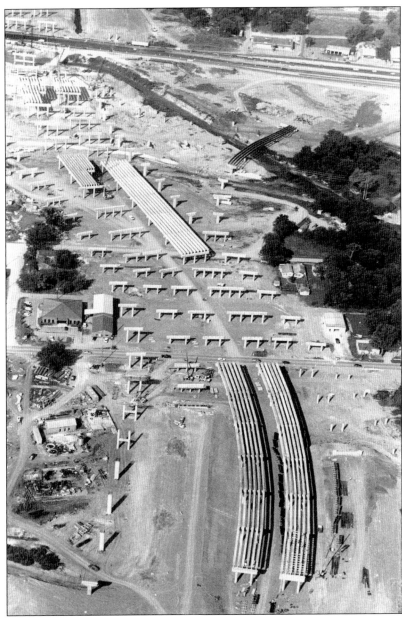

Eventually, modern development overtook many historical sites and treasures in and around Huntsville. When a proposed interstate highway threatened to destroy Huntsville's historic railroad depot in the 1980s, dedicated historic preservationists rallied to save the 1860s-era building. Now a city museum, the historic Huntsville Depot is a testament to the importance of history in the city. This 1989 photograph shows Interstate 565 under construction near downtown Huntsville. Although many buildings were saved from destruction, hundreds of other buildings and historic sites were lost in the name of urban renewal and highway construction. The raised highways that now ring Huntsville have made travel easier as the city grows outward. Unfortunately, much of the natural beauty and early flow of downtown Huntsville has been lost to modern development. Historic preservationists continue to fight to protect Huntsville's past, and photographs such as this are reminders that there is still much work to be done.

Two

THE HUSTLE AND BUSTLE
OF HUNTSVILLE

Huntsville's residents worked hard to create a town and then a city. The local population nearly tripled, increasing not only in number but in diversity as well. Civic culture greatly expanded when more people moved to Huntsville. Many of the new residents engaged in different civic activities, including Boy Scouts and Girl Scouts, Kiwanis, theater, and local bands. They also joined different levels of the new and growing local government. The whole infrastructure of the city had to be rethought. The influx of traffic brought demand for new construction projects: homes, roads, and a revamping of the school system. The economy quickly industrialized, and Huntsville became a regional economic and social leader in the Tennessee River Valley.

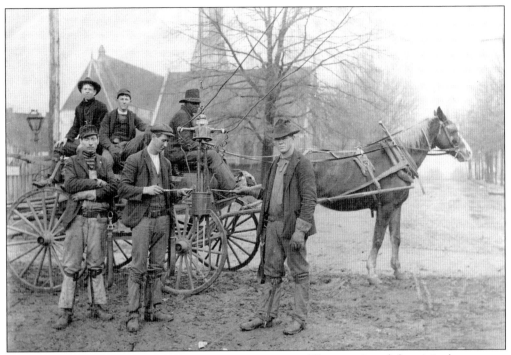

The promise of electricity became a reality on May 10, 1887, after city leaders signed a contract for an Indianapolis firm to install 32 streetlights and 300 incandescent bulbs. The contract also called for the firm to double the electrical capacity of the city if demand made further improvements necessary. Above, workers in climbing gear pause for a photograph after stringing line in Huntsville.

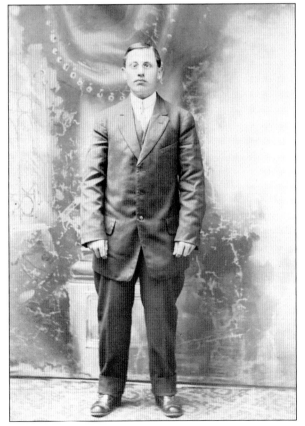

Blindness did not stop Charlie Thomas Lacy from learning how to use a dial phone in 10 minutes and becoming the full-time operator of the telephone exchange in Huntsville. Lacy was born on June 8, 1886, and died on February 9, 1961. He and his wife, Myrtle Hill, had one daughter, Hazel Lacy Roberts.

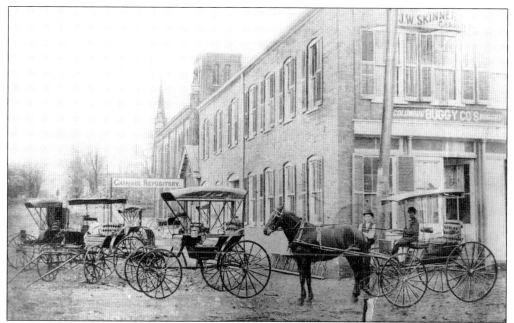

J.W. Skinner Carriage Repository, seen here in 1890, sold buggies like these on the corner of Greene Street until 1909. Skinner failed to make the transition from horse-drawn carriages to automobiles and soon lost business to competitors. Early automobile manufacturers such as Ford and General Motors transformed modern cities by building affordable cars that allowed people to live in the suburbs and commute to work.

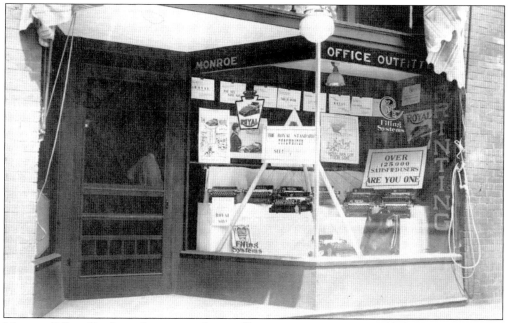

Monroe Office Outfitters began supplying office equipment to Huntsville businesses in 1923. The Royal typewriter became an essential part of many professional offices. Office efficiency and automation became important elements of the modern workday. Note the Royal advertisements directed at women in the front window display.

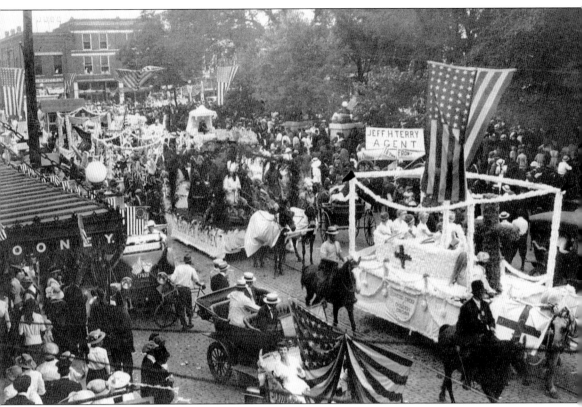

This parade on Courthouse Square includes a collection of people, cars, buggies, and horse-drawn floats. The lead float is that of the Order of the Golden Cross, which admitted men and women between the ages of 16 and 55. The order has its origins in freemasonry and provided life insurance benefits to its members. The central membership requirement was the agreement to abstain from alcoholic beverages. Behind the Golden Cross float is a sign saying, "Jeff H. Terry, Agent." In the 1899 city directory, Terry is listed a salesman at T.T. Terry, but by the 1920s, he was the second vice president of Farmers State Bank. He went on to be the vice president of Holmes-Terry Realty in the 1930s. Parades and rallies were common events in downtown Huntsville.

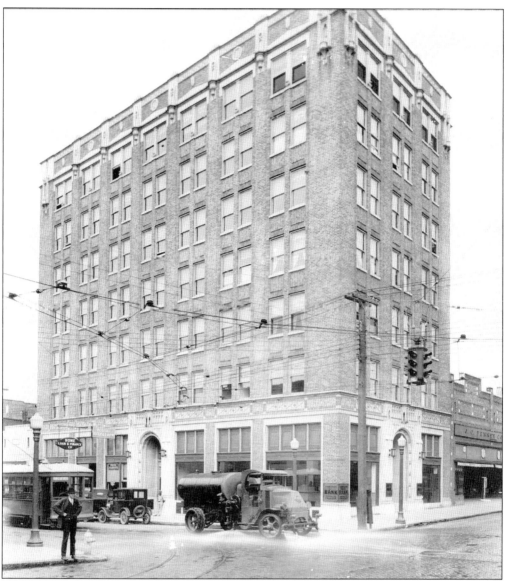

The Hutchens Building with its recognizable frog gargoyles sits at the corner of Jefferson Street and Clinton Avenue. Work on the building began in 1925. The *Huntsville Daily Times* reported that 500-watt electric lamps lit the construction site so workers could work day and night on the seven-story "skyscraper." Its completion was front-page news on June 6, 1926. The building was designed by R.H. Hunt of Chattanooga and built by Earl Cline of Birmingham. The construction foreman told a reporter, "Full ten hours constitute a day's work, including Saturday, which is payday." The building was the new home of Tennessee Valley Bank, which received a total of $80,000 in deposits on opening day. In 1944, Ira Terry and the Hutchens brothers, Vernon, Morton, and Willard, purchased the building and continued to use it as office space. Preservationists added the building to the National Register of Historic Places in 1980.

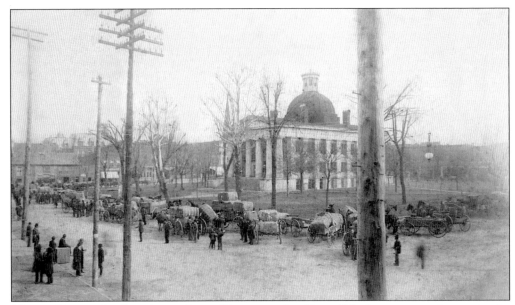

"Cotton Day on the Courthouse Square" became a familiar call for busy cotton planters in the 1800s and early 1900s. Madison County farmers produced 30,000 bales of cotton for market by 1910. Local cotton mills and factories operated more than 230,000 spindles and needed more than 60,000 bales of cotton to keep up with commercial demand.

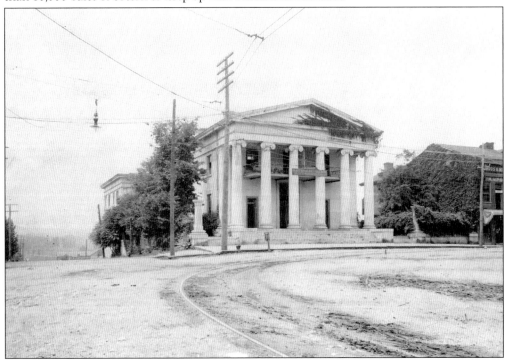

The First National Bank witnessed many of downtown Huntsville's historic milestones, including the paving of streets, the installation of the first electrical wires, and the first city stoplight. Take time to walk downtown and compare this 1920 photograph to what it looks like now; note the rolling hills and trees in the background, in what is now Big Spring International Park.

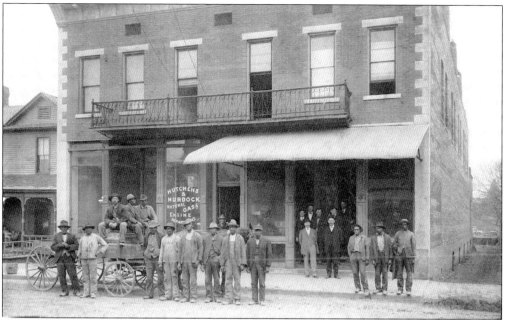

The Hutchens & Murdock Natural Gas and Engine Department was on West Holmes Avenue. This unique photograph shows both black and white workers gathered in front of the business. Also, note the advertisement on the side of the building. The sides of buildings often served as convenient and noticeable backdrops for painted advertisements in the era before large billboards in open fields.

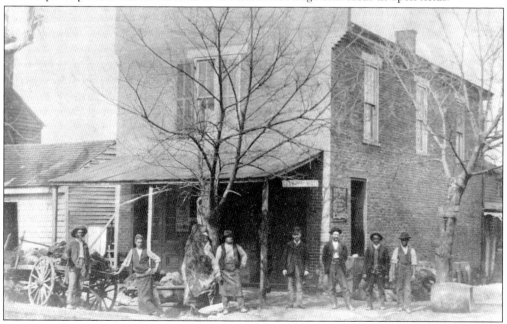

Although Huntsville had become a modern city by 1900, many vestiges of its past still existed in the downtown area. Wind and Company, run by Mr. I. Wind, collected animal hides and wool on North Washington Street near what is now Dunavant's Corner. These workers rendered hides collected from local farmers and hunters. Wind and Company was the only business of this type in Huntsville in 1900.

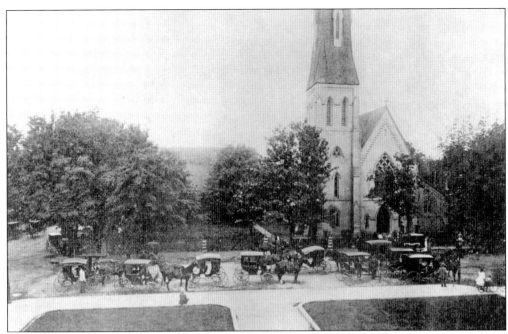

New churches appeared along Huntsville's streets as more people moved into the area. The Church of the Nativity has served Episcopalians since 1859. The church is seen here during the funeral of Rev. John Monroe Bannister on March 29, 1907. Bannister graduated from Princeton University and moved to Huntsville, where he served local Episcopalians from 1860 to 1906.

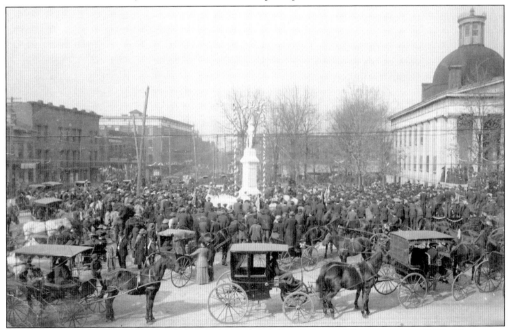

A large crowd turned out for the dedication of the Confederate Monument in 1905. Musicians and visitors packed the Huntsville Hotel (left foreground) and the McGee Hotel, on the next street corner. This photograph was taken looking down Jefferson Street just before a large fire swept through the downtown area.

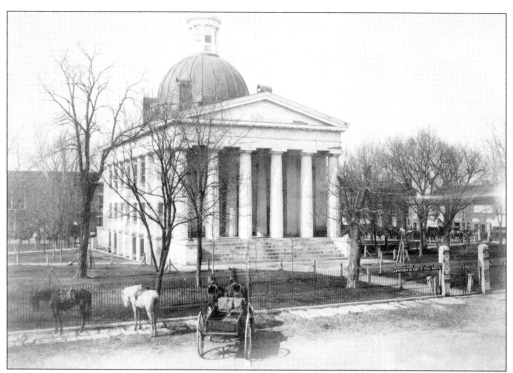

George Steele's original courthouse was beginning to show its age and lack of upkeep by the late 1800s (above). This beautiful courthouse served as the foundation of downtown Huntsville, but overuse and the lack of upkeep sometimes made it a risky visit. Witnesses reported that overflowing spittoons and tobacco juice forced the building to be closed for a day for cleanup. Horses hitched too closely to the gated entrances of the courthouse also made it a risky walk for many visitors. The iron fence seen here was removed in 1924. The interior of the probate office and some of its staff members are seen below. A handwritten note on the back of the photograph identifies the man with the mustache as Orville B. Laxsen.

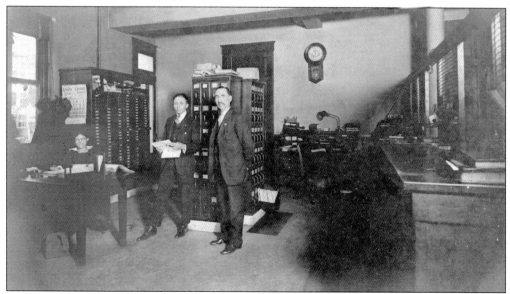

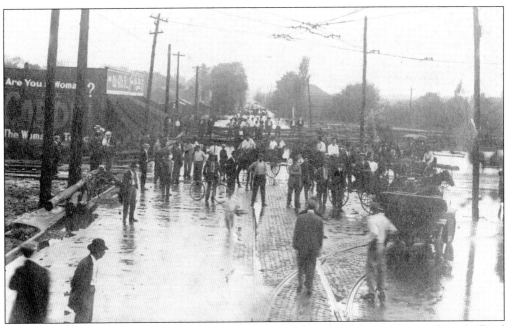

This photograph was taken on September 22, 1912, the day after a devastating and costly flood hit the city. A foot of rain fell between Saturday night and Sunday morning. Note the different modes of transportation in this photograph. City residents could walk, bike, ride a horse or wagon, drive a car, or take the streetcar during this transitional period in Huntsville's development.

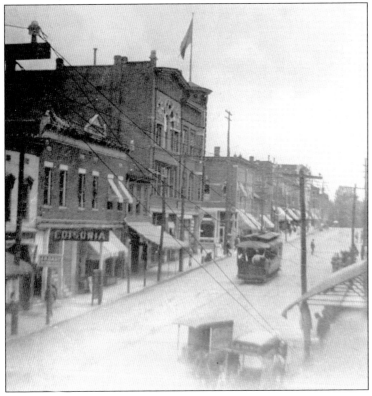

Early streetcars made it easier for city residents to travel to any part of the city, and many of them enjoyed taking trips to the movies. Movie fans could take the trolley to the Edsonia Theater on Washington Street to see a movie for 5¢. Note the tangle of electrical wires that now marked Huntsville's landscape; compare these scenes with earlier photographs that predated electricity.

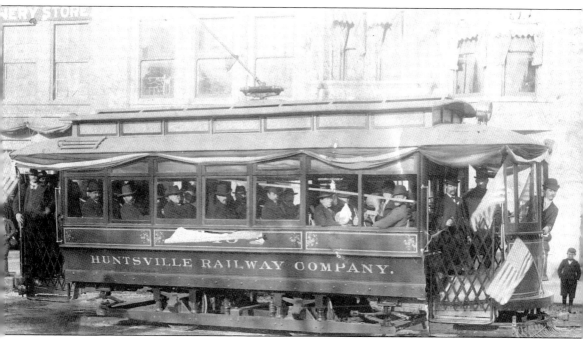

In 1900, Cyrus F. Sugg amassed enough stock in the Huntsville Electric Company to become its sole owner. He later sold it to the Huntsville Railway Light and Power Company. Huntsville citizens had been unimpressed with the dependability of the old electric system and welcomed the change in ownership. The original caption attached to this photograph reads, "Dedication of Huntsville's first electric streetcar February 27, 1901. In the car are seated Mayor Tom Smith, members of the Board of Aldermen, and members of Monroe's Band." The first streetcar left the station at 2:00 p.m. Mr. Snickenberger, who had been in charge of setting up the machinery and the steam plant, operated the car, and C.F. Corfield, who oversaw the laying of the track, acted as conductor. On June 15, 1915, Alabama Power Company purchased the Huntsville Railway Light and Power Company. Electric streetcars served Huntsville residents until buses became popular in 1931.

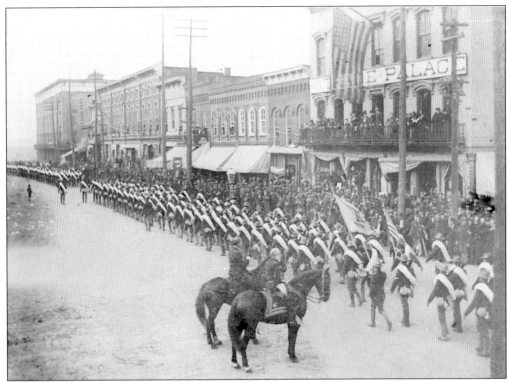

In 1898, residents of Huntsville witnessed federal soldiers invading their downtown once again, as 18,000 troops under the command of Gen. Joseph Wheeler encamped in and near the city. Local residents presented the ex-Confederate officer with a fine horse for his military service during the Spanish-American War. This photograph was taken from the northern side of Courthouse Square.

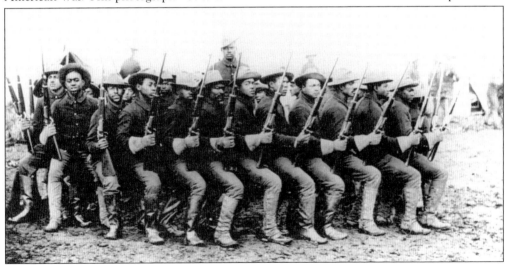

This photograph highlights some of the buffalo soldiers who fought in the Spanish-American War and were stationed in Huntsville. A monument to these men was erected at the Cavalry Hills Academy for Academics and Arts School in 2009. Huntsville's monument is the only one of its kind east of the Mississippi River. Cavalry Hills is named in honor of the 10th United States Cavalry Regiment.

Three

Enjoying Life in Huntsville

Huntsville was not all work and no play; there have always been many activities around the city for citizens to participate in. Early on, circuses, theater troupes, and menageries visited Huntsville and brought joy to both children and adults. The surrounding landscape also created many outdoor activities for the community. The rolling hills have provided plenty of scenic land for cyclists to enjoy riding their bicycles. The waters around Huntsville, including the Tennessee River and Lake Guntersville, have provided Huntsvillians with great fishing, swimming, and boating opportunities. Huntsville has also had many other activities and civic organizations throughout the years, which have helped keep people active in the community.

Huntsville also has a host of parks, golf courses, and public activities, including the performing and visual arts, many festivals, and church activities for people to enjoy. Sports in particular have always been a favorite pastime for Huntsville natives. In the 1920s, baseball was so popular that some stores would close early when the Huntsville Independents played games against rivals from other towns or cities. Friendly competition amongst local sports teams, whether between local schools or teams in different mill villages, has helped keep Huntsville a tight-knit community.

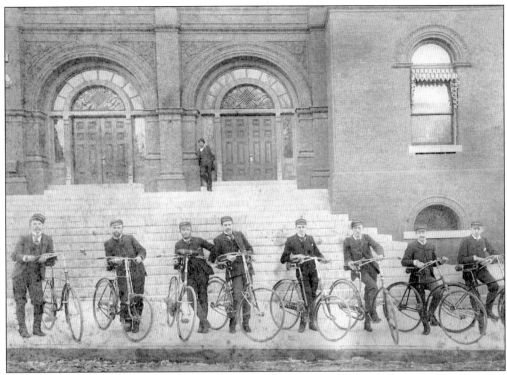

Members of the Spring City Cycle Club posed proudly with their bikes in front of the Schuadies Building, on the corner of Madison Street and Courthouse Square, in the late 1800s. In 1892, biking became so popular in the city that Huntsville's city council had to pass an ordinance to keep bicyclists off sidewalks.

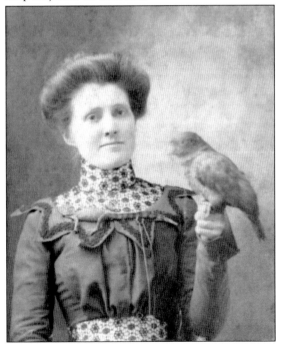

Early city residents, like many modern Americans, enjoyed the company of pets as companions and friends. Here, a professional photographer captured Ellen Bartee Cary posing with her parrot and alligator. The alligator rests on Cary's chest and is attached to her dress with a hook through a chain around its tail. This photograph was taken around 1900.

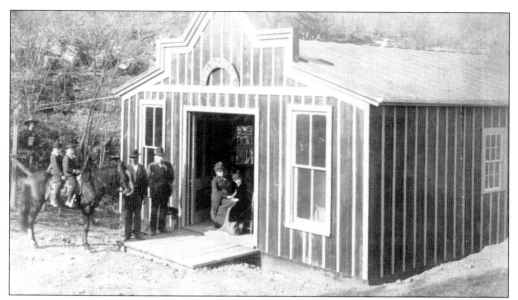

In 1888, Henry Fuller of Ohio moved to Huntsville and bought 11 acres of land that included an extensive cave system directly under the city. Fuller, seen here with his family, opened the caves to the public in April 1890 after installing electricity, a rail system, boats, and a large dance hall for visitors.

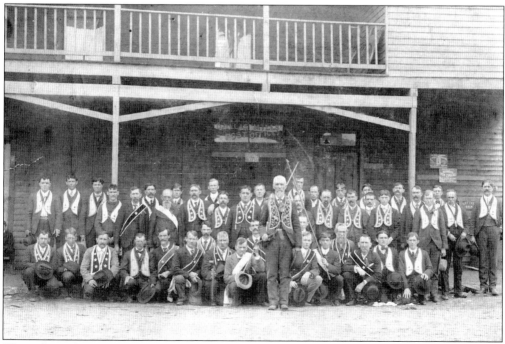

The Independent Order of Odd Fellows of Huntsville posed for this group portrait in front of the Dallas Mills post office in the late 1800s. Civic clubs and fraternal organizations became popular in Huntsville as people searched for social, religious, and cultural connections with others living in the city.

45

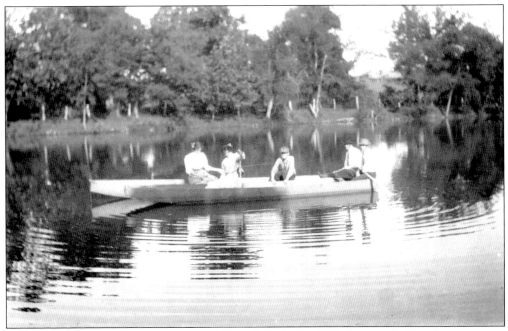

Several young people pose in a rowboat on Mastin Lake in this 1913 photograph. The close proximity of rivers and lakes made boating a popular activity for locals. Over the course of time, water has served as a source of nourishment, transportation, and entertainment for city residents.

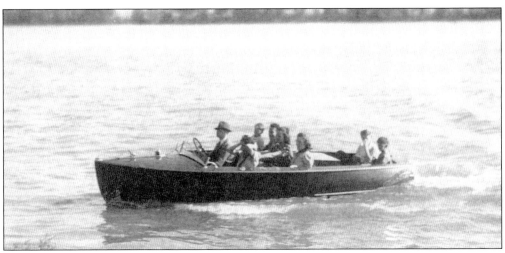

Gene Monroe introduced the first motorboat, or pleasure boat, to Huntsville in 1939. The boat is most likely a Hacker-Craft speedboat manufactured in Michigan. Monroe was the grandson of popular Huntsville bandleader D.C. Monroe. Boating would become more popular among city residents after the Tennessee Valley Authority created new lakes and deeper rivers by building dams and locks on the nearby Tennessee River.

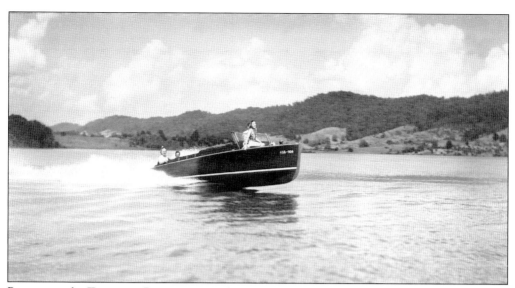

Boaters on the Tennessee River enjoy a ride in an early speedboat along the undeveloped shores of Madison County. Huntsville's Marina Park, located near Ditto's Landing, is still a popular attraction and is enjoyed by boating enthusiasts today. This area also became popular with hikers, fishermen, bird-watching enthusiasts, and picnickers.

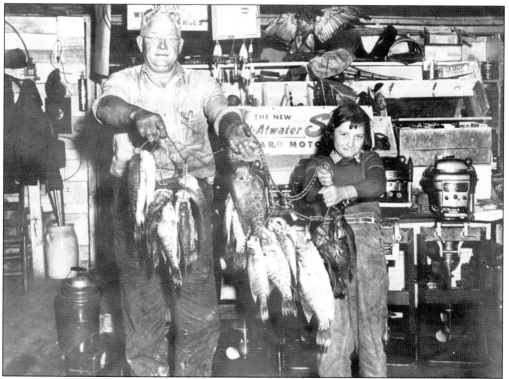

Fishing was and is popular with residents of all ages. Well-stocked lakes and streams meant that a grandfather and his grandchild could spend a fruitful day on the water. The outboard motors and other supplies for sale suggest that this photograph was taken in a fishing shop after a successful day on the water.

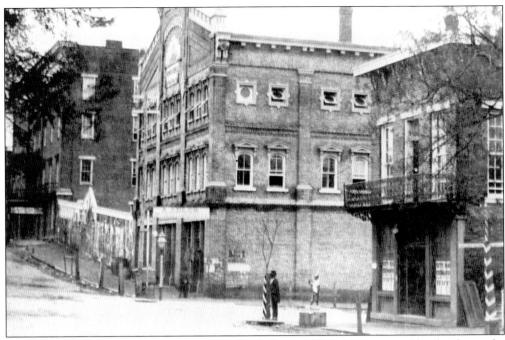

The tradition of opera in Huntsville began after LeRoy and Judith Pope set aside a land trust for the establishment of an opera house in 1825. In 1872, the Huntsville Opera House opened on Jefferson Street to wonderful reviews. The building could seat 1,200 guests and was considered an architectural highlight of downtown Huntsville. Unfortunately, fire destroyed the building on November 5, 1911.

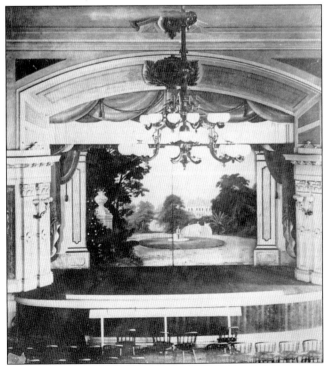

The stage and orchestra pit of the opera house are seen here in the 1890s. The opera house hosted a variety of acts, including Blind Tom, a former slave and autistic savant; the Irish Brigade Band and Orchestra; the Payson English Opera Company; and Healy's Hibernian Minstrels. On April 12, 1894, Helen Keller and her companion, Annie Sullivan, performed to a sold-out audience.

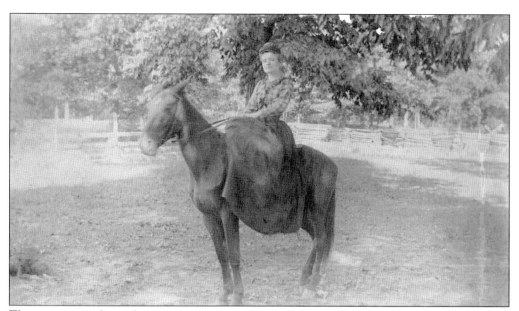

This woman is elegantly attired in a riding habit while posing sidesaddle. Horseback riding was a popular pastime in the city, and Huntsville had a long tradition of horse racing; several famous horses ended up in city stables, including legendary horses Gray Gander, Telemachus, and Cyclops. Andrew Jackson spent considerable time and money on horses in Huntsville and often visited the city.

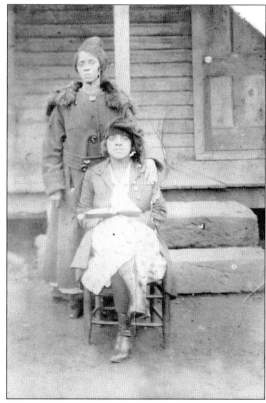

Traveling photographers often passed through Huntsville and took photographs of city residents. These two unidentified ladies posed for the camera wearing their nicest outfits. The seated woman proudly holds a book, highlighting yet another form of leisure among city residents, reading.

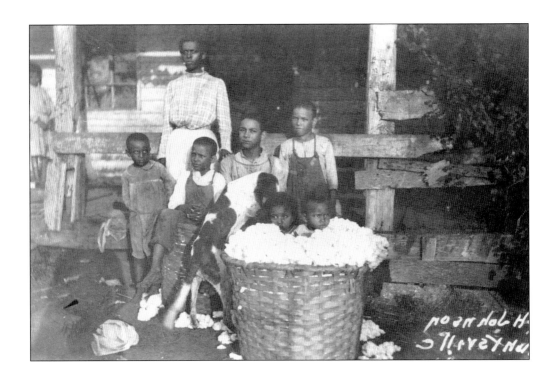

Fresh-picked cotton served as a source of fun for city children in this early 1900s photograph. Baskets such as the one above were often used for the cotton-picking season, which lasted from late September to early December. Below, the Monroe children pose with their pet goat. The younger child is eating Kellogg's cereal from the goat's dish while the older child sits on her small cart. In an era before video games and other modern distractions, city children learned to play outside with toys fashioned from everyday life. These two photographs highlight the joy of childhood in Huntsville.

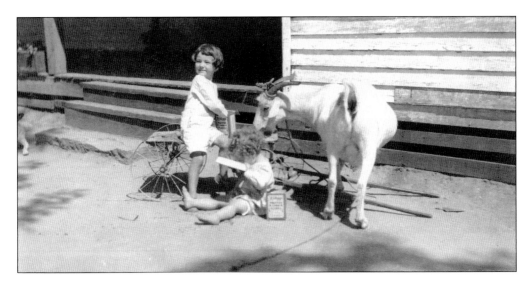

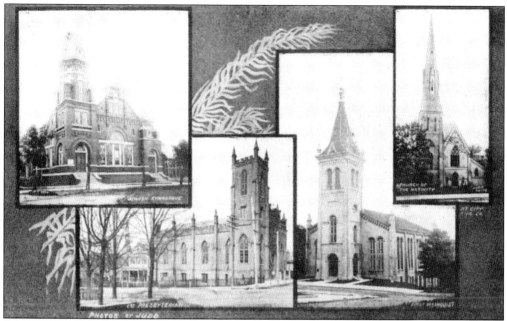

Huntsville boasted many beautiful churches in the historical downtown Twickenham area. Church life offered residents an enjoyable sense of fellowship. These photographs were included in many of the early print publications used to publicize the fine things Huntsville and Madison County had to offer. Souvenir books were also made available to passers-by, highlighting what townspeople considered to be quintessential elements of the area, such as the fact that Big Spring produced 24 million gallons of water a day. The souvenir books also celebrated its past of social refinement and elegant homes. The Jewish synagogue, Temple B'nai Shalom, is featured above alongside the First Presbyterian Church, the First Methodist Church, and the Church of the Nativity. The photograph below features the Presbyterian Church, the First Baptist Church, and the Saint Mary of Visitation Catholic Church.

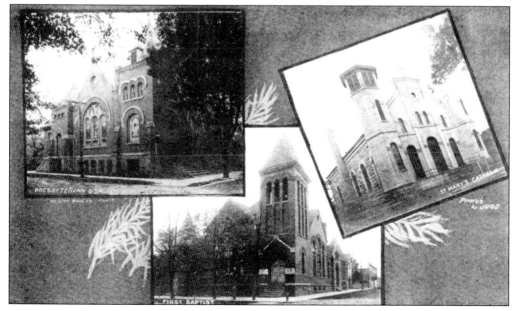

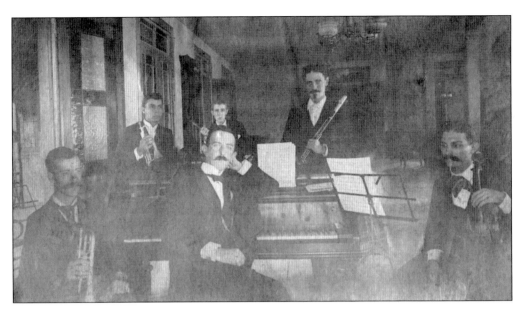

Monte Sano, or the "Mountain of Health," has been a recreational draw for city residents since the first settlers moved to Huntsville. The North Alabama Improvement Company and city leaders developed the Monte Sano Railway line in 1886 so city residents could visit the new hotel on the peak of the mountain. Visitors would leave from a station on Jefferson Street and take the seven-mile trip to the top of the mountain. Once there, they could relax outside in the natural beauty of the mountain and then later enjoy a sense of cultural refinement, with music and entertainment in the evening. Above, a band poses in a rare interior view of the Monte Sano Hotel. Below is violinist C.R. Klenk, who was reportedly asked to play with the Boston Symphony Orchestra.

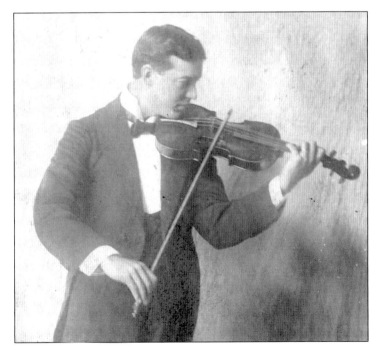

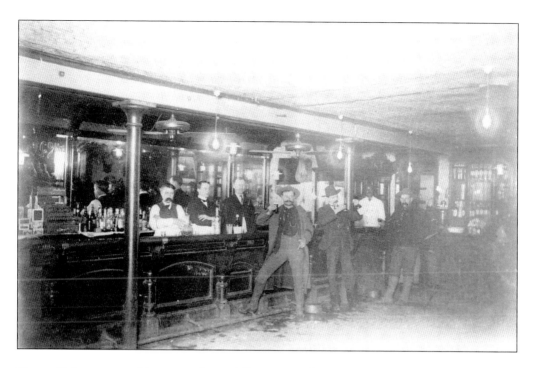

Huntsville's taverns and bars served up a different sort of entertainment for city residents. These two photographs highlight the rough nature of early drinking establishments in the city. Above, a patron props his foot up for a drink while others toast the photographer in the Huntsville Hotel bar in 1899. The bar attendants are dressed in proper coats and vests. The photograph below shows a more relaxed scene in J.E. Payne and Company Saloon. Note that both bars had large spittoons for their guests—and it appears that many of them had bad aim.

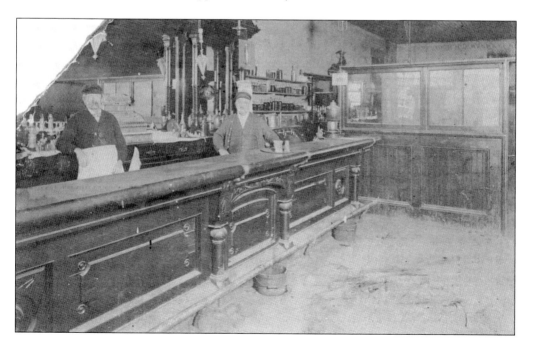

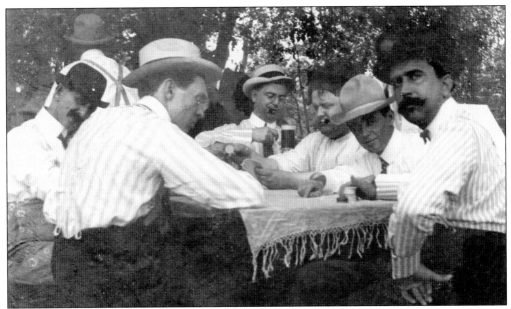

Some early city residents enjoy cold beer and cigars while playing cards. Such public scenes of drinking, smoking, and gambling became less acceptable as reformers tried to clean up the bad habits of Americans. In 1925, at the height of the Roaring Twenties, a group of investors broke ground for the Huntsville Country Club. Private clubs became havens for people looking for a drink during Prohibition.

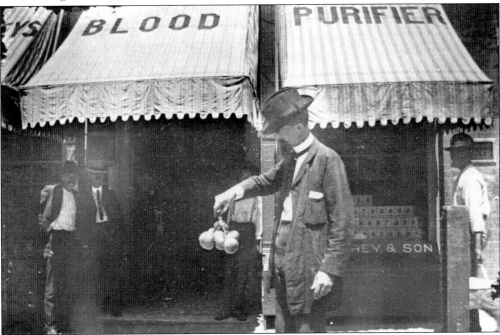

This gentleman stands in front of the Humphrey and Son drugstore on Washington Street in downtown Huntsville. He appears to be displaying a fine grouping of apples. Passers-by and onlookers have stopped and turned to look at the spectacle. The awning of the drugstore adds interest with its "Blood Purifier" advertisement.

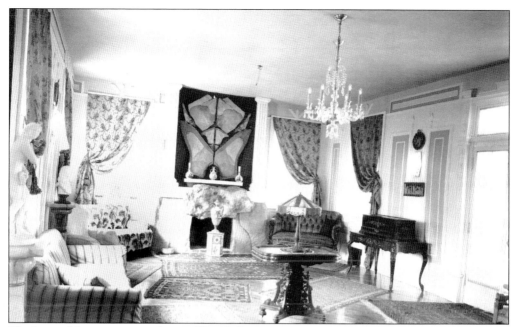

The beautiful mountain residence of Dr. William Henry Burritt was left to the city of Huntsville in 1955. It was turned into a museum featuring a historic park with log cabins from the 1800s. The mansion itself is built in the shape of a cross, and the walls are insulated with hay. Burritt on the Mountain continues today as one of Huntsville's favorite tourist destinations.

On August 16, 1950, the *Tuscaloosa News* reported that Huntsville was a "tennis-mad" town and that residents were looking forward to the first Huntsville Open. Tennis players from around the Southeast signed up for the event. Seen here from left to right are 1953 winner Wade Herron, runner-up Gordon Warden, and Milton K. Cummings.

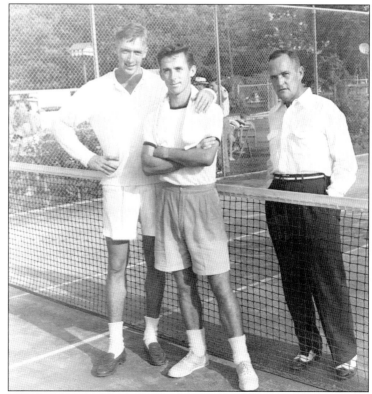

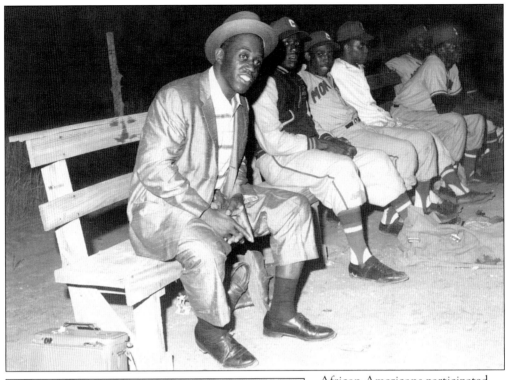

African Americans participated in integrated baseball in the late 1800s until racism and Jim Crow laws forced black players out of white leagues by 1900. Black players then formed their own independent teams and went "barnstorming" around the United States. By 1920, an organized league structure was formed and Negro League baseball enjoyed wide success all over the United States until the 1960s. Huntsville Optimist Park is one of the last remaining ballparks where Negro League teams played, and is still used today. Three of the players above are, from far left to right, Ted Rasberry, Sam Allen, and Eugene Scruggs. Local promoters often treated fans to performances between innings. At left, the Flying Nesbits pose for a publicity photograph. The group became well known in Huntsville and around the South.

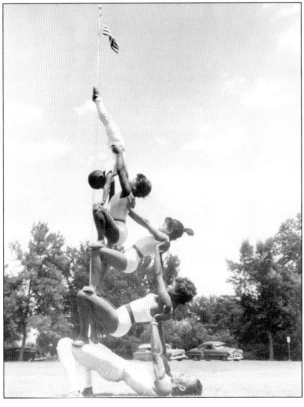

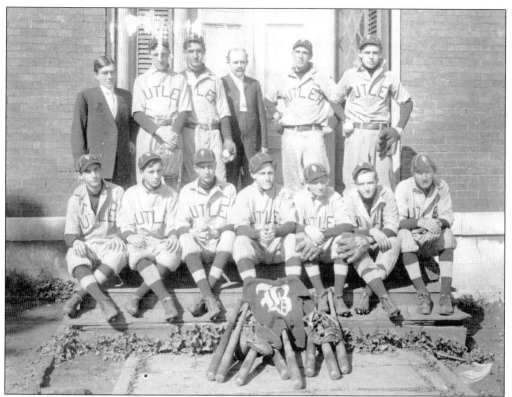

Baseball served as a popular activity and pastime for the people of Huntsville. Here, a group of young men on the Butler team pose with owner Samuel R. Butler in 1908. Local businessmen often purchased teams as a form of advertisement.

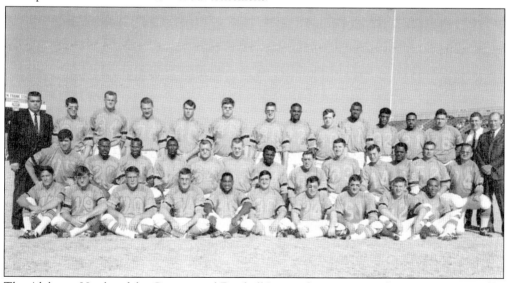

The Alabama Hawks of the Continental Football League became a popular team in Huntsville. The city team eventually became known as the Huntsville Hawks and played their games at Milton Frank Stadium. Despite good local support for the team, the league folded in 1969. The stadium scoreboard is on the left.

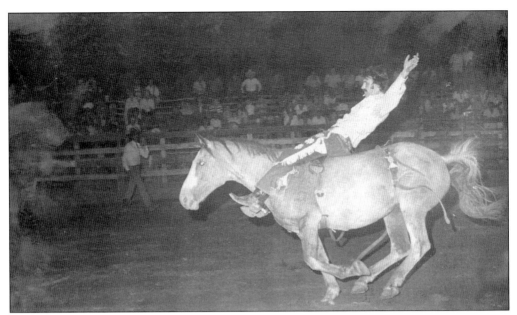

Wild West shows and traveling rodeos have entertained Huntsville residents since the late 1800s. These shows often combined theatrics, comedy, and genuine competition in order to draw large crowds. These two photographs illustrate the combination of daring horsemanship and humorous showmanship involved. Cars, buses, and trolleys had pushed horses out of downtown Huntsville long before, but these shows allowed guests to harken back to a more rural time. As modern tastes changed, however, shows like these began to disappear altogether. Downtown Huntsville still hosts a yearly circus, and residents can catch glimpses of exotic animals and performers at the historic Huntsville Depot.

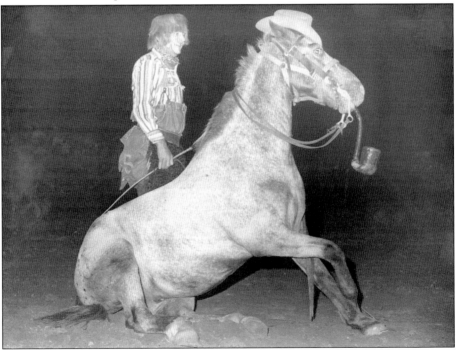

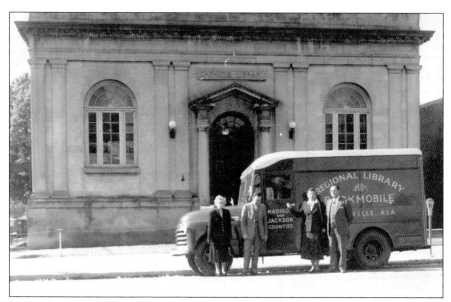

The Huntsville–Madison County Public Library is the oldest continuous library in Alabama. While it was still part of the Mississippi Territory, the *Huntsville Republican* reported, "Never was the liberality of the citizens of Huntsville and its vicinity so cheerfully exercised as on a late application to them to contribute to the establishment of a Public Library." The library had numerous locations over the years, but that changed when the Huntsville Carnegie Library (above) opened on February 29, 1916. The library system quickly grew, adding new branches and a bookmobile. Books on the road became popular and the library expanded its region to include surrounding counties and towns. During construction of the Guntersville Dam, the Tennessee Valley Authority requested that the Huntsville bookmobile provide service to Guntersville and lend books to their employees. In 1952, the library returned to exclusively serving Madison County. Unfortunately, the city tore down the Huntsville Carnegie Library, building a parking lot in its place.

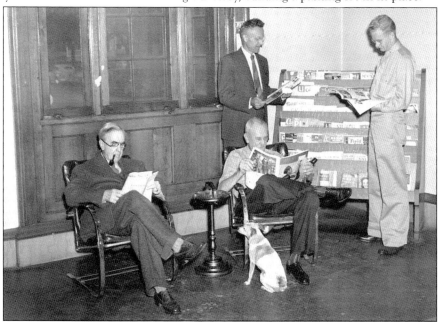

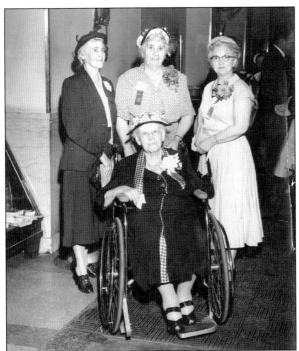

Members of the Huntsville library board are seen here with Francis Jones (seated), the children's librarian. Board members include, from left to right (standing) Mary R. Davis, the chairman of the board; Mamie Terry; and Annie Chase. This photograph was taken in the lobby of the Russel Erskine Hotel on Clinton Avenue.

On May 31, 1940, the Huntsville public library opened a branch for African Americans in the basement of the Lakeside Methodist Church on Jefferson Street. Dulcina DeBerry served as the first African American librarian in Madison County at a time when separate but equal was anything but equal in Huntsville.

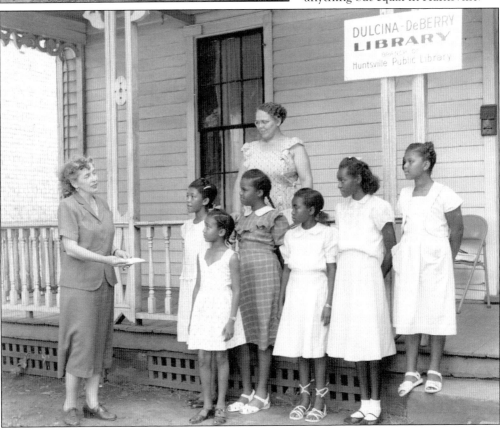

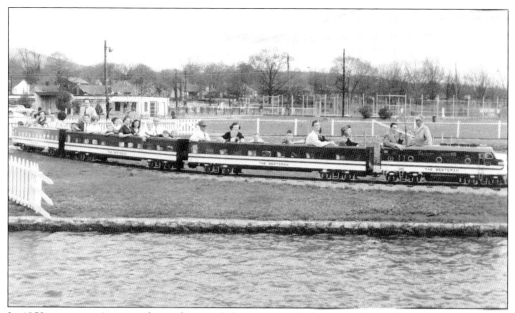

In 1953, concerned city residents chartered the Sertoma Club to provide employment opportunities for local teenagers by forming a "Youth Employment Service." The club also sponsored the Sertoma Club train in Big Spring Park. This photograph shows a group of parents and their children on the train. In 1966, as downtown space became more valuable, the train was moved to Braham Spring Park.

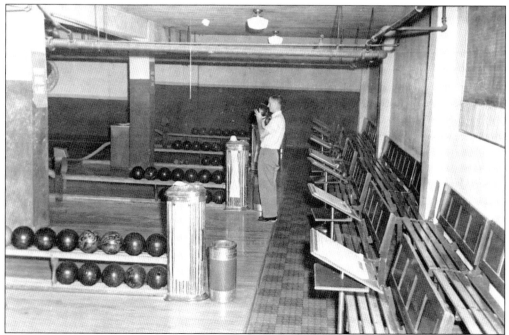

This bowling alley was in the basement of the Times Building, at the corner of Holmes Avenue and Greene Street. Judge William Page, a longtime Huntsville resident, remembers that it cost 25¢ to bowl. It was not an automatic bowling alley; as pins were knocked down, they were reset by hand. Judge Page also recalls an upstairs café that served "the best pimento and cheese in the world."

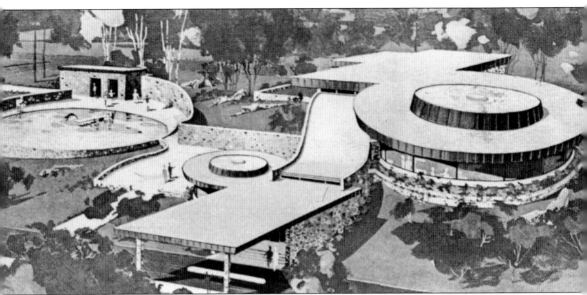

Overlooking southwestern Huntsville on Golf Road, this building has served as a modern nightclub for more than three decades. In the late 1960s, the Golf Road area began to experience a burst of apartment complex developments that were convenient to the parkway and to Municipal Golf Course, at the end of the road. Construction of Parkway Country Club began on April 15, 1962, and a charter membership cost $300. The architect of the recognizable building was Lloyd H. Kranert. By 1968, it had become the Dinner Plantation Theater, which hosted professional off-Broadway shows. In 1971, it turned into the VIP Dinner Theater. Over the years, it has gone through various nightclub incarnations, including disco, country, gay, hip-hop, and techno. In 1973, a devastating fire ripped through the building and closed it. The circular architectural details survived the fire and remain recognizable features for city residents.

Four

LEARNING IN HUNTSVILLE

Huntsville schools began to appear throughout the city as settlers moved into the area. The earliest schools were separated by gender. Boys were taught reading, writing, arithmetic, and foreign languages. Girls were taught the basics, along with embroidery and patchwork. In 1812, territorial legislature was passed stating that a public school, Green Academy, would be built in Huntsville. No money was allotted for the school however, so the trustees had to raise money by a lottery. The school was burned down during the Civil War.

Religious institutions or individuals were responsible for opening many of the private schools in Huntsville, including Monte Sano Female Academy, Huntsville Female Seminary, and the Bascom Institute (later Huntsville Female College). Huntsville Female Seminary and Huntsville Female College were confiscated by Union troops during the Civil War and used as hospitals. Reconstruction brought about yet another change in public education, with freedman's schools constructed to educate newly freed slaves. Rust School was one of the first freedman's schools to open in Huntsville. While private education thrived before and after the war, many children did not have the opportunity to attend school. The shift to public school systems started with Reconstruction.

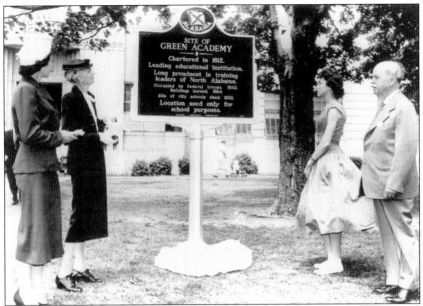

The first schools in Huntsville were small private schools and academies. Boys and girls had separate schools, and the newspapers were filled with advertisements and announcements for them. One of the earliest schools was the Green Academy, established after the territorial legislature of Mississippi passed an act on November 25, 1812, declaring, "There shall be established in Madison County an academy which shall bear the name Greene Academy."

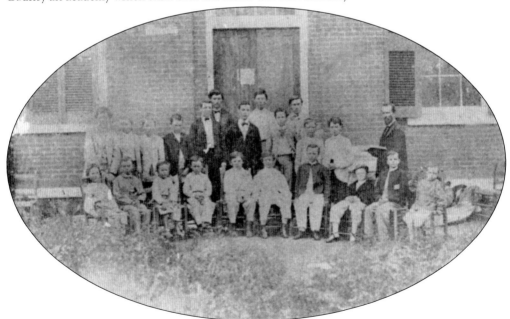

School trustees were allowed to raise money by running a public lottery. Gen. John Brahan donated the land where East Clinton School now stands. On November 7, 1823, the *Huntsville Democrat* noted, "Greene Academy is located in a handsome grove about a quarter mile east of Huntsville." There are no photographs of the early school, but this is thought to be an early photograph of professor Charles O. Sheppard and his students.

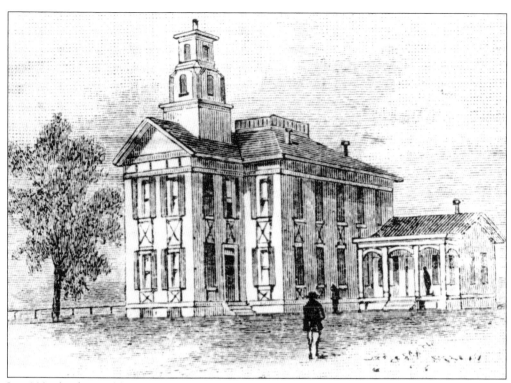

In 1883, the first public school in Huntsville (above) was built on the site of Green Academy and opened to city residents. James Hutchens won the bid to build the school at a cost of $4,000. Many people, if they could afford it, still preferred to send their children to private schools or have private tutors. Mary Clay had a well-respected small private school on Eustis Street, offering her pupils basic reading, writing, and arithmetic as well as French, dancing, voice, and piano. Below, the children dance around the festive pole in celebration of May Day.

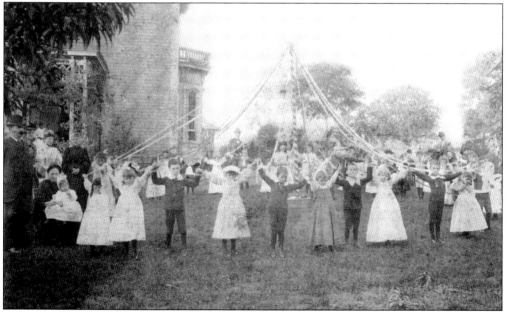

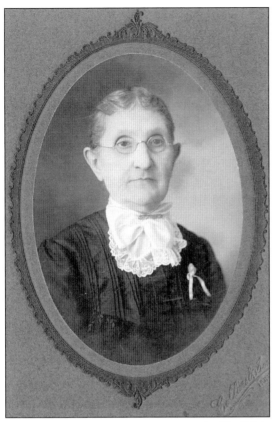

Fanny Taliaferro, seen at left in 1906, had all the qualities of a traditional schoolmarm: a dark dress, a white starched collar and brooch, and spectacles. The handwritten caption on the back of the photograph below refers to the school on East Clinton Street as a "state school." The 1899 Huntsville city directory referred to it as "the Huntsville Public School." Samuel R. Butler was the principal, and the school had 10 teachers. There was also a public school on O'Shaughnessy Street, with two teachers on staff. Most teachers in the early 1900s were female and well trained. Note that none of the children in the first row have shoes on.

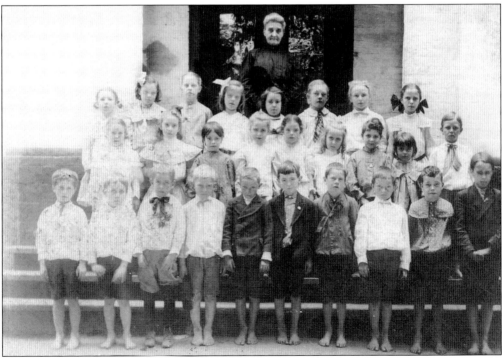

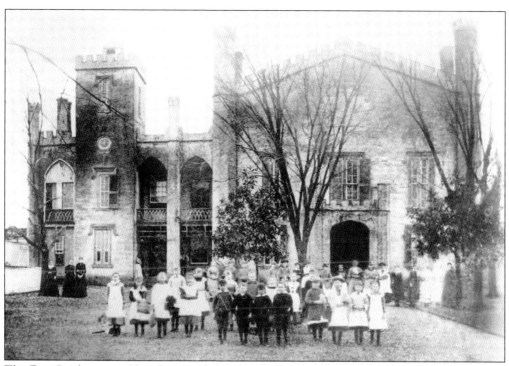

The First Presbyterian Church opened the Huntsville Female Seminary in 1831. Church elders hired teachers who had been trained with the Beecher Philosophy of Education in Hartford, Connecticut. Katherine Beecher, the sister of Harriet Beecher Stowe, became a noted educator in the early 1800s, and sent several teachers to Huntsville. The motto of the seminary was "to develop all that is good in mind and heart; and to suppress all that is evil; to nurture the moral and physical, as well as the intellectual powers; to form the true woman, as well as the accomplished lady." The interior of the seminary is seen below. Note the gaslight fixtures extending from the center of the ceiling.

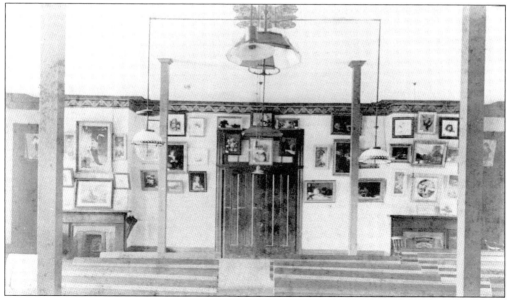

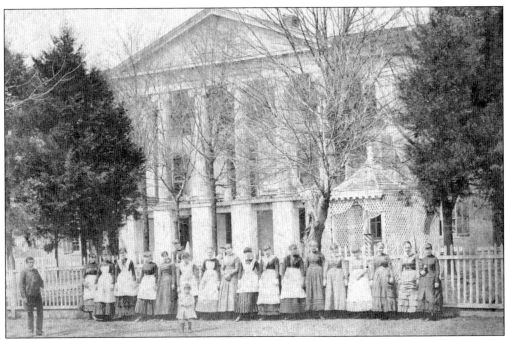

The Huntsville Female College's school motto promised "that our Daughters may be as Cornerstones Polished after the Similitude of a Palace." The college (above), established by the Methodist Church in 1851, was on Randolph Street, just down the road from the Huntsville Female Seminary. Initially, the building had two stories, but a third was added to accommodate increased enrollment. George Steele's unique design for the college reportedly included dumbwaiters in each of the bedrooms. The seminary and the college were both boarding schools, although boarding was not a requirement. The college was used as a hospital during the Civil War but reopened as a school after the war ended. In 1959, a group of 17 former students posed together for the group photograph below during the unveiling of the state historical marker where the college once stood.

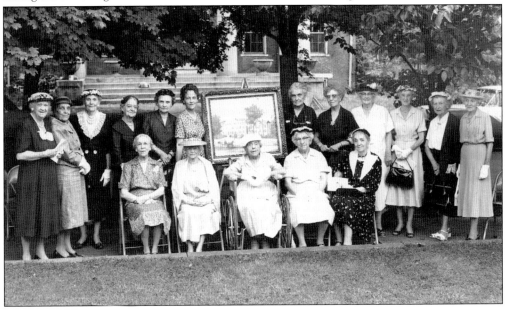

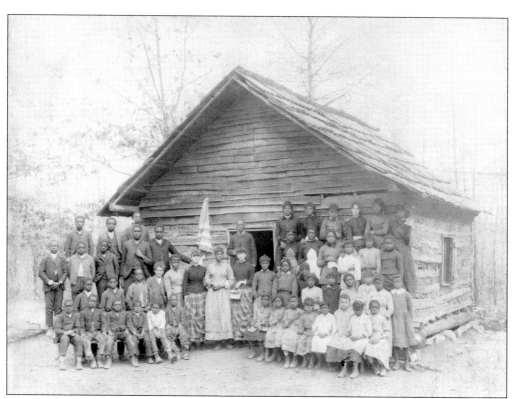

Educational opportunities for African Americans after the Civil War centered around the development of freedmen's schools. These schools taught an estimated 100,000 former slaves to read and write. In 1870, the Rust School on Franklin Street (pictured at right) was one of the first freedmen's schools to open in Huntsville. On August 20, 1869, the *Huntsville Weekly News* reported that the school had been named for Dr. Rust, who had been a driving force behind the establishment of the school. "The Freedmen's Aid Society, aided by the Government, has nearly completed a beautiful and commodious brick edifice," it reported. "Now fill your beautiful school with the most promising youth of your State. Educate teachers for your schools all over the State."

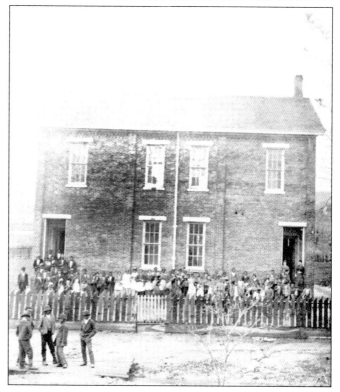

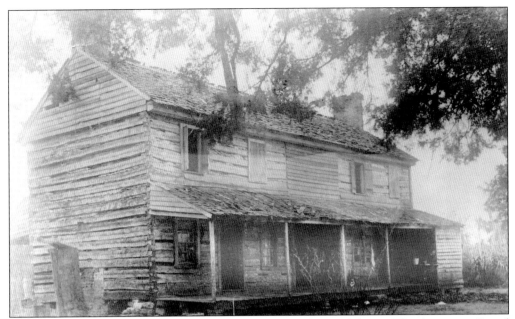

A Cherokee mission school also served students in northern Alabama. The American Board of Commissioners erected this building in March 1820 for Foreign Missions of the Presbyterian Church in America. Rev. Daniel S. Buttrick was the first teacher and administrator. The school was closed after Pres. Andrew Jackson signed the Indian Removal Act into law in 1830.

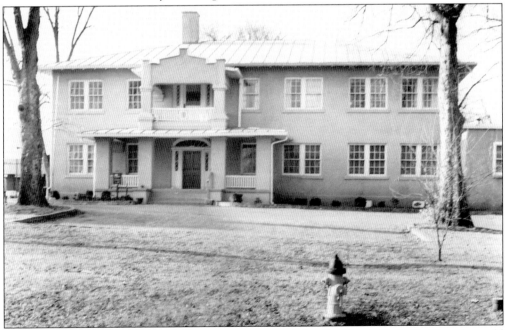

On November 7, 1900, the *Weekly Democrat* announced that St. Mary's Catholic Church would open a parochial school under the auspices of the Sisters of Loretto. In addition to its high academic standards, the Loretto Academy became known for its elaborate graduation ceremonies. With an orchestra, orations, and dance and theatrical performances, its commencement was known to last more than three hours. The school charged admission for the performance.

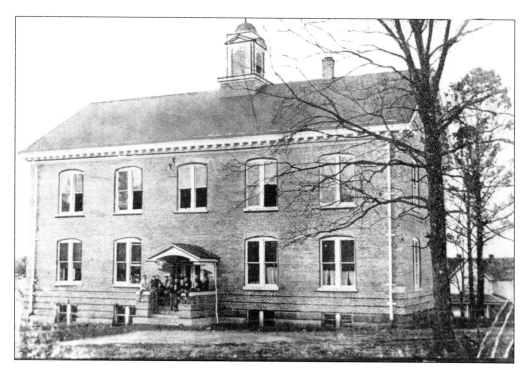

Samuel R. Butler established Butler Training School (above) in the early 1900s, later selling it to J.C. Goodrich, who had taught Latin and mathematics at the school. Eventually, new investors purchased the building, and it became known as the Will-Taylor School by 1921. The school promised, "Honesty-Perseverance-Friendliness: We believe these are the essential traits of character necessary for a young man or young woman to have in order to make a really successful career." The yearbook, *The Wist*, featured candid shots of students such as the one below. The school building later became the Huntsville Junior High School and is now the Annie Merts Center.

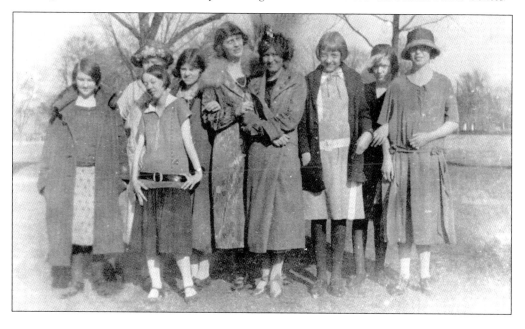

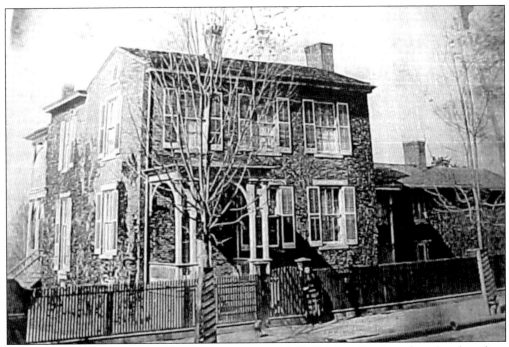

In early March 1880, the *Huntsville Advocate* announced, "A Teacher's Institute for colored teachers was formed." D.S. Brandon—who went on to be one of the first African Americans elected, along with T.W. Townsend, to Huntsville's board of alderman—came to the school from the Rust School. A year later, in 1881, the property was purchased to build the Colored Normal School at Huntsville (above). It was located on West Clinton Street and established by William Hooper Councill in 1875. In 1890, the school became a land-grant institution, the State Agricultural and Mechanical College for Negroes (below, now Alabama A&M University).

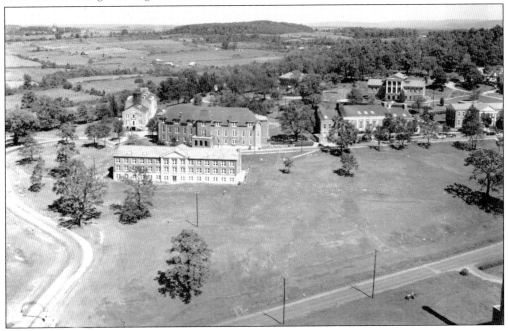

William Hooper Councill served as the first president of Alabama A&M, from 1890 to 1909. Councill was born into slavery in Fayetteville, North Carolina, in 1848. He was brought to Huntsville by David C. Humphrey, who eventually freed him before the end of the Civil War. Councill attended a freedmen's school in Stevenson, Alabama, and then returned to Huntsville to start a school in 1869. He became a respected African American city leader during a time when "separate but equal" and the violence of Jim Crow ruled Alabama.

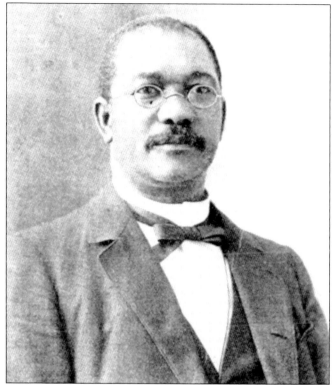

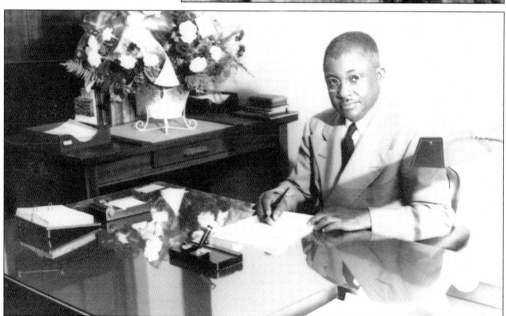

Dr. Joseph Fanning Drake served as president of Alabama A&M University from 1927 to 1962. When school leaders feared an impending closure, Drake said, "I did not come here to conduct the funeral of A&M." In fact, he did the opposite, and university supporters often called him "the savior." Drake oversaw the construction of multiple buildings and the addition of 616.13 acres of land to the campus. Later, the J.F. Drake State Technical College was named in his honor.

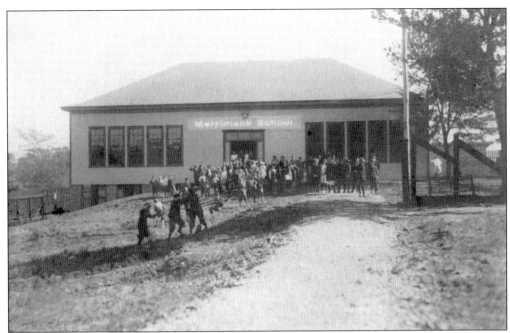

Merrimack Manufacturing Company built the wood-frame school building above in 1910. It had four classrooms, large windows, and a spacious schoolyard. Prior to the construction of this school, the children attended classes in a room above the mill store. Local children had to attend school for six to eight weeks a year. In 1919, the mill began to expand its facilities and built a new school, a beautiful brick building, the interior of which is seen below. It was named Joe Bradley School in honor of Joseph J. Bradley Sr. In 1951, Bradley School graduated its last senior class. The mill also expanded the old mill store building, which became known as Merrimack Hall in 1920.

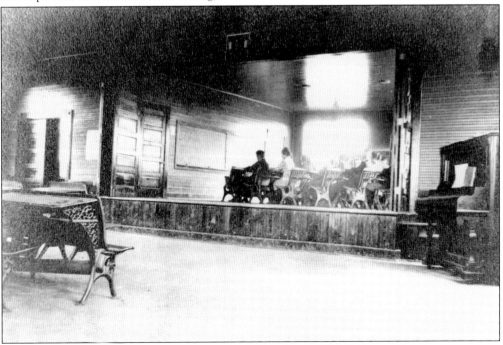

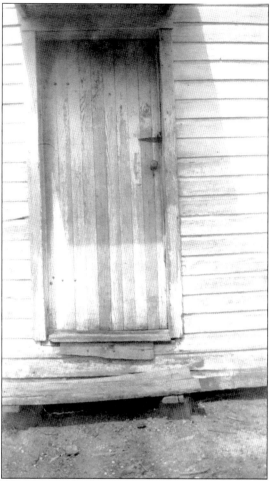

"Knock! And it shall be opened" was the original handwritten caption of the photograph at right. It also could have been the motto of Pine Grove School, Madison County's first Rosenwald school. Started by Booker T. Washington and sponsored by Julius Rosenwald in the early 1900s, the Rosenwald school program built 4,977 schools in 15 states for African American communities. Below, James and Willie B. Martin pose next to a parked car in front of Pine Grove School. Rosenwald schools offered what Alabama's white-controlled school systems would not: a chance for African American students to attend school and learn.

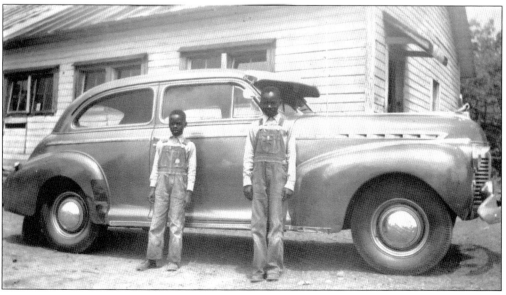

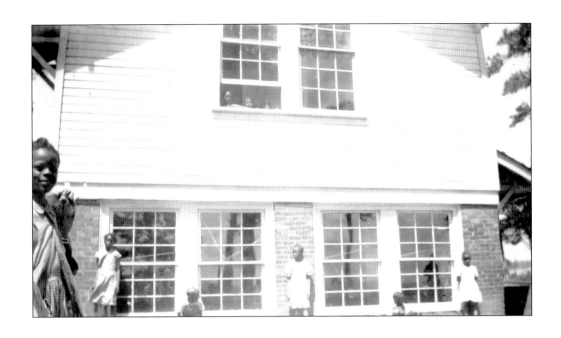

Booker T. Washington used money from Julius Rosenwald to open six small schools in rural Alabama. These schools were completed by 1914 and served as the beginning of a larger movement of school construction. In Huntsville, the Mount Carmel School (above), a two-story wood-and-brick schoolhouse, was built between Ryland Road and Winchester Road in 1913. School administrators added a third room in 1930 for a total cost of $1,050. Below, a group of students gather for a class photograph in front of the older St. James School.

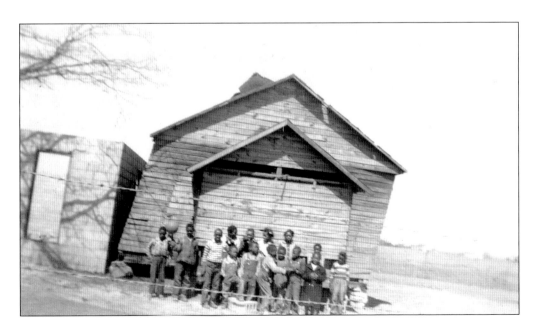

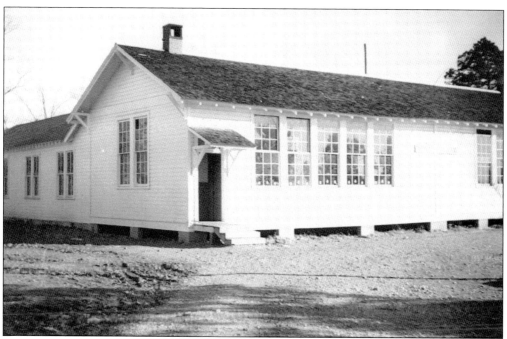

The Farmers Capital School, seen in both these photographs, also served African American students after its completion in 1928. The one-room schoolhouse sat on two acres and was heated by a potbelly stove provided by Madison County. Local residents had to raise matching funds for the building, and in time, African American contributors gave $900, the general public donated $450, and a county school fund chipped in $200 for the construction of the school. One teacher taught all of the primary grades, and eventually a second room was added to the building. Although the Rosenwald school program ended in 1932, its legacy in Huntsville continued long after the last school closed.

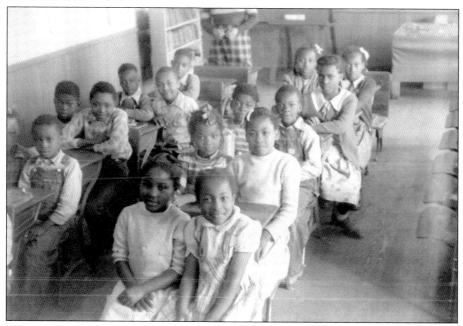

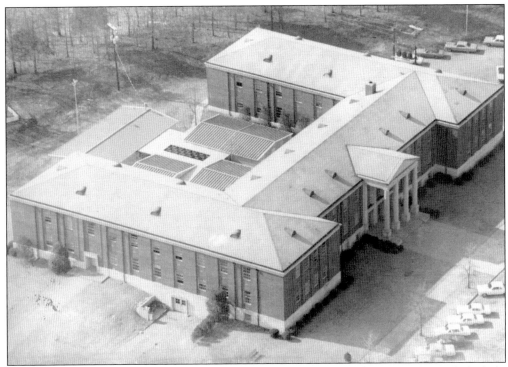

The University of Alabama in Huntsville (UAH) began with 139 students in 1950. With the help of German scientist Dr. Wernher von Braun and Huntsville native Dr. Francis Roberts, UAH became an important legacy of the city's past and present interest in higher education. In 1961, Morton Hall (above) became the icon of the new university. In the rear of Morton Hall, a small white picket fence protects Perkins Cemetery. Among those buried there is Capt. Llewellyn Jones, a Revolutionary War soldier and survivor of Valley Forge. The old concrete UAH sign below on Holmes Avenue has now been moved to the center of campus so students can paint the letters to reflect their moods, announce events, or show school pride.

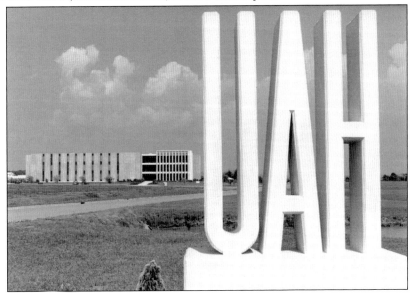

Five

MILLS AND VILLAGES
IN HUNTSVILLE

In the 1920s, Huntsville became the leading cotton cultivator in Alabama as well as the top textile manufacturer. Mills in Huntsville employed hundreds of people, including children. The major mills in Huntsville were built in the late 1800s, and as time passed, they were converted from using steam to more efficient sources of power. Mill villages built homes to house their employees and offered everything needed to survive, including grocery stores, schools, libraries, recreation centers, churches, and theaters. While most villagers did not have time to socialize after working and completing household chores, mill villages were tight-knit communities where people looked after one another.

Mills brought about a generation of hard-working children, as child labor was not yet regulated and children as young as seven went to work in the mills. In order to work in the mills, children had to be at least 12 years old, but parents often lied, swearing that children were of "mill age" on release affidavits so their children could go to work early. Children were required to go to school at least eight weeks per year to be eligible to work in the mills. If they did not do this, they were put on a list of ineligible workers.

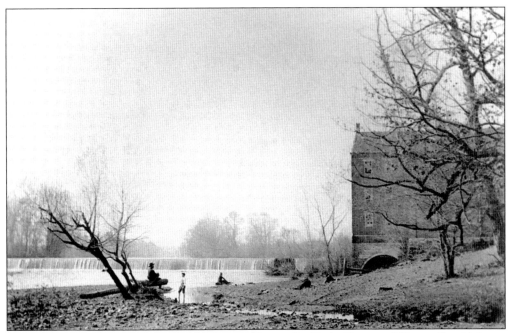

Edward Chambers Betts's 1909 book *Historic Huntsville: Early History of Huntsville, Alabama* is often quoted for its description of the Bell factory as the "most noteworthy single industrial development of the times." Officially incorporated in 1832, the Bell factory was 10 miles northeast of Huntsville near the Three Forks of the Flint River. Since the mill was water powered, there was no steam whistle; a simple bell called employees to work, lunch breaks, and quitting time. Manned with skilled slave labor, the Bell factory had 100 looms and 3,000 spindles in the mid-1800s. The original structure burned in 1841 and was rebuilt with the buildings in these two photographs. The mill ceased operations in 1885. All that remains today are a few foundation stones and the dam. The child in the foreground below is thought to be George McLaughlin.

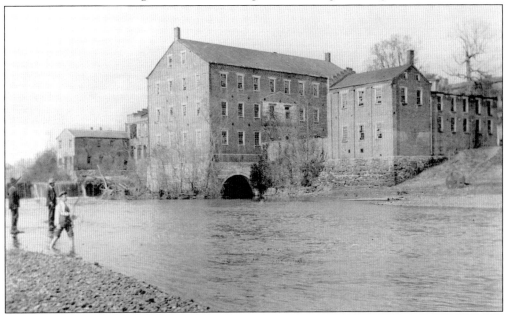

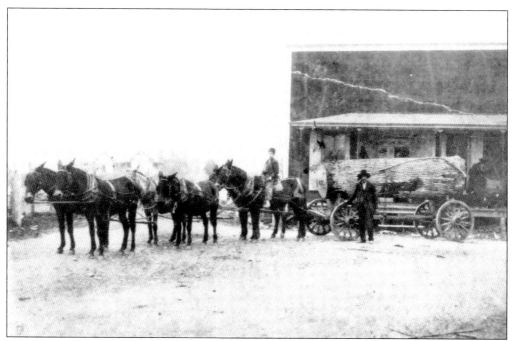

The handwritten inscription on the back of this photograph reads, "The largest log hauled out of New Hope." Local residents brought the log to Dan Calvin Drakes's gristmill in New Hope, just outside of Huntsville. Logs this size were common in the late 1800s, and local timber fueled a building boom in the growing city of Huntsville.

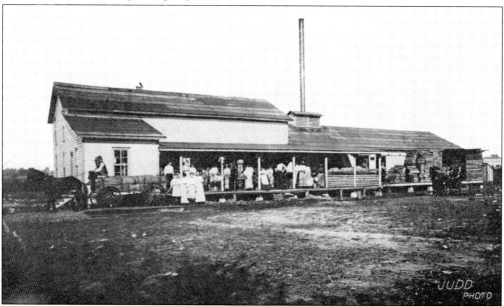

Huntsville's industrial sector grew as the city developed in the late 1800s. In 1908, the Businessmen's League of Huntsville used this photograph of the Huntsville canning factory to highlight a sense of progress in the city. The league's brochure lists 56 different mills, foundries, factories, and cotton gins, as well as six nurseries, one of which was proudly hailed as the largest wholesale nursery in the country at that time.

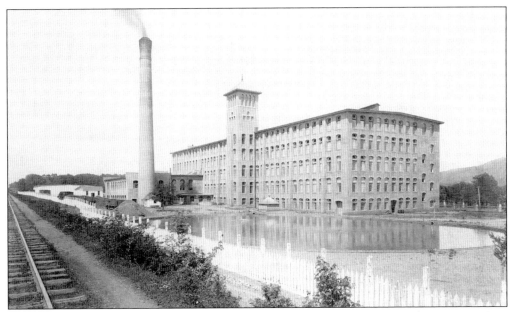

Dallas Manufacturing Company finished this massive building on Oakwood Avenue in East Huntsville in 1892. The Boston-based architectural firm Lockwood, Green & Company was hired for the project. The plant contained 25,000 spindles and 750 broad looms. At the time, the mill produced the widest cotton sheeting in America and shipped products as far away as China.

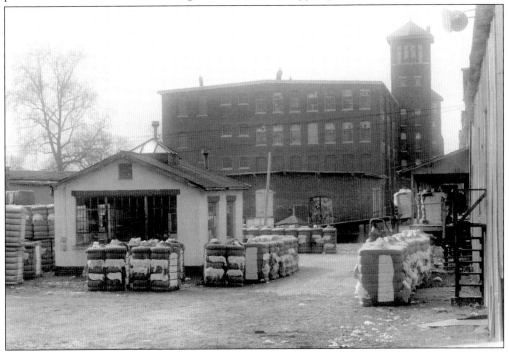

This photograph of the Dallas mill features a rare view of the warehouse area as well as the grading and weighing house, surrounded by bales of cotton. After 58 years of producing and processing cotton, the mill ceased operation in 1949 and was sold by its stockholders to two businessmen from Boaz for $175,000.

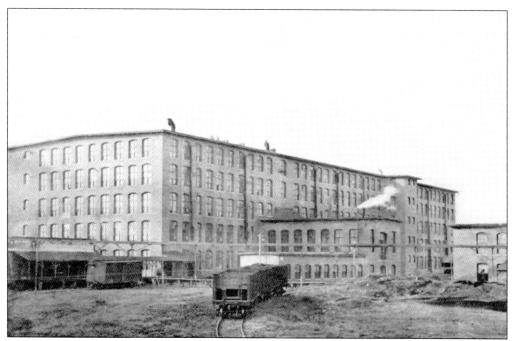

Merrimack Manufacturing, of Lowell, Massachusetts, opened a mill in Huntsville in 1900. The company had a capital stock of $4.4 million and 100,000 spindles. The mill advertisements stated that it manufactured print cloth, organdies, percales, and madras. This photograph was the featured centerfold panorama in the 1908 Businessmen's League of Huntsville brochure.

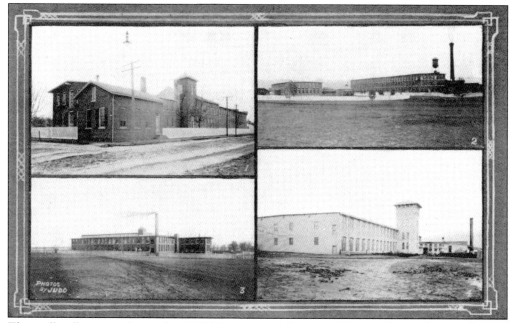

This mill collage was also in the 1908 Businessmen's League of Huntsville brochure. It features four of the smaller mills in the city, clockwise from top left: Huntsville Cotton Mills, Lowe Cotton Mills, Abingdon Cotton Mills, and Huntsville Knitting Mills. The pictures were chosen for publicity reasons; note the black smoke coming out of the towers as a sign of productivity.

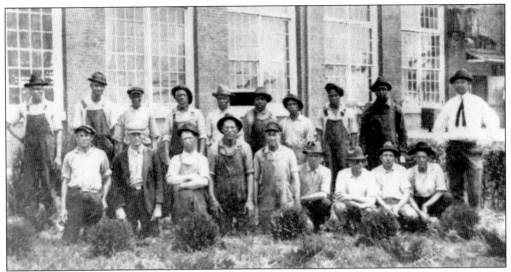

Many people found easy employment and made the move from farm to factory after Huntsville's textile industry grew in the early 1900s. Although wages were generally low, most factory workers found it better than working on the farm. In a 1949 *Huntsville Times* article about her days at the Dallas mill, A.D. Bowers remembered making $14 in her first month of employment. Many women and children worked in these mills and were often paid less than men. The handwritten caption on the back of the group photograph above says that this assembly of 1898 Dallas mill loom-fixers and dolphers worked 11 hours a day. Children earned 25¢ a day and men made between 75¢ and $1. The 1925 photograph of Lowe Mill below shows a biracial workforce in the mill's dye room.

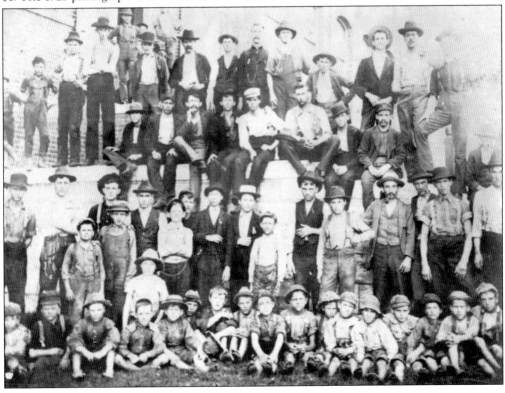

Noted photographer Lewis Hine was hired by the National Child Labor Committee to investigate the realities of America's working children. He made three visits to Huntsville, first in November 1910 and then again in November and December 1913. The photograph at right of 10-year-old Charlie Foster was taken in 1910. It has been a focal point of interest and was used as inspiration for the play *Upon Their Shoulders: The Merrimack Mill Story.* When Foster's descendants learned of the existence of the photograph, one of his relatives said, "Charlie died at age 64 from multiple sclerosis and was buried in his overhauls." Children in the mills, like the ones below, were mostly dolphers or spinners. The youngest children were sweepers and were responsible for sweeping up lint.

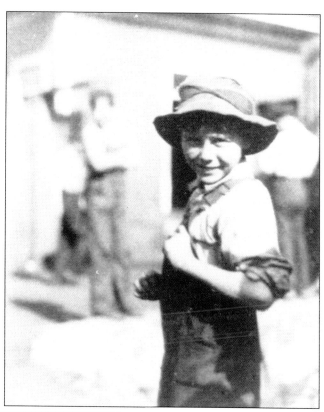

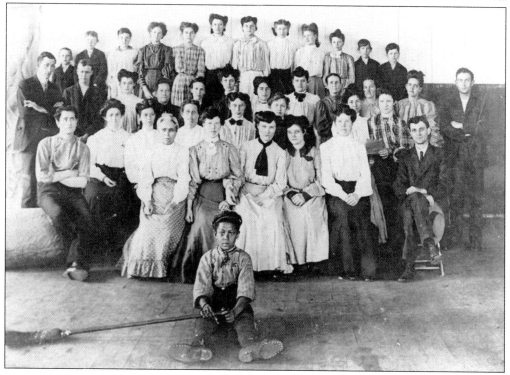

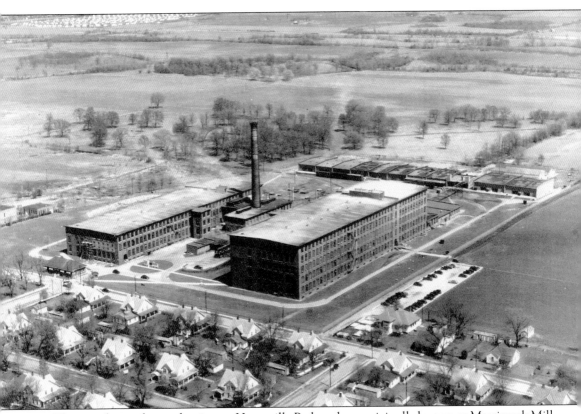

This aerial view shows what is now Huntsville Park and was originally known as Merrimack Mill and Village on Triana Avenue. As the mills grew, so too did the mill villages, which became the focal point of life for mill families. The mill village was an all-encompassing lifestyle. The historian Wayne Flynt explained, "It was theoretically possible that a man's mother might attend a pre-natal clinic established by the mill, that the baby be born in a mill-owned hospital and delivered by a mill-paid doctor, that he be educated in a mill-supported school, married in a mill-subsidized church to a girl he met in the mill, and when he died be buried in a coffin supplied at cost, by the mill in a mill owned cemetery."

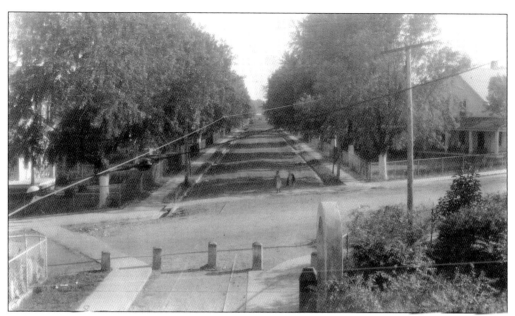

Before the introduction of the streetcar, the Merrimack and Dallas mill villages were isolated communities on opposite ends of Huntsville. The electric streetcar helped to bring the mill villages in touch with the city, as it ran from Merrimack Village through downtown Huntsville and on to Dallas Village. In the photograph above of South Alpine Street, two people walk toward the streetcar stop, where it reversed and started back to town. One of Huntsville's first streetcars is seen below with the conductor and an advertisement that reads, "Bargains in Wallpaper, the People's Store." Streetcars were used extensively in the city from February 27, 1901, to February 23, 1931.

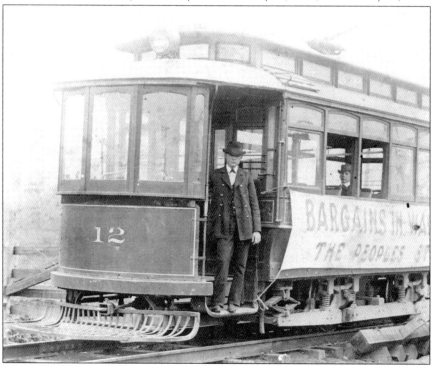

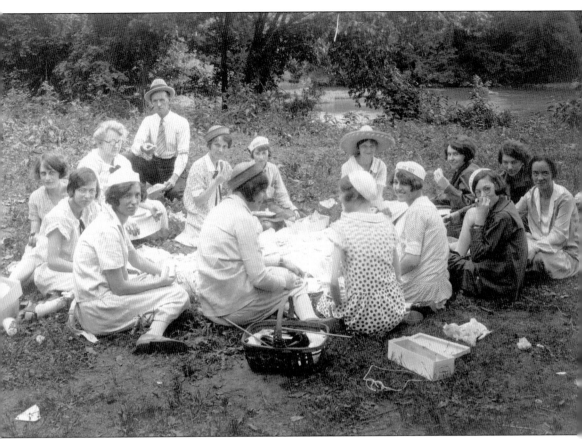

This group of teachers from Joe Bradley School picnic along the banks of the Flint River in 1925. Joe Bradley School was a celebrated example of mill village education. The Merrimack Mill School went through several phases but eventually became most recognizable as Joe Bradley School. Built in 1919 for mill village children, the school was named after Joseph J. Bradley Sr., the managing agent of the Merrimack Mill from 1905 to 1922. The school had all grades and eventually offered night classes for adults. The school auditorium was built in 1928. Some of the teachers seen here are Annie Bradshaw Clopton (back left, left of the man in the straw hat), a celebrated cobweb artist and early Girl Scout organizer; Mary Esslinger (back middle, in sombrero), who taught music; and Mabel Hughes (front left, in little white hat), who taught first grade for more than 40 years.

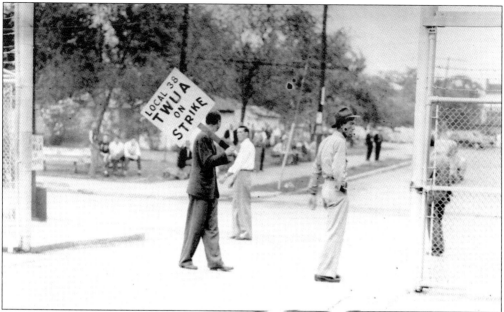

In oral history interviews conducted by local historians, many people recall fondly their time in the city's mill villages, where they thought of their neighbors as an extended family. Some historians, however, note that at times these neighbors more resembled a dysfunctional family than friendly neighbors. In 1934, John Dean helped the United Textile Workers organize strikes and picket lines in Huntsville, ushering in the modern era of labor strife in Alabama. The 1951 Textile Workers Union of America strike was a regional strike involving 40,000 textile workers, with mills in Virginia, Louisiana, Alabama, North Carolina, South Carolina, and Tennessee participating. Mill workers asked for a 22-percent wage increase after negotiations broke down between mill owners and Congress of Industrial Organizations representatives in Washington, DC. Despite widespread unrest, only four textile mills in Alabama joined the strike.

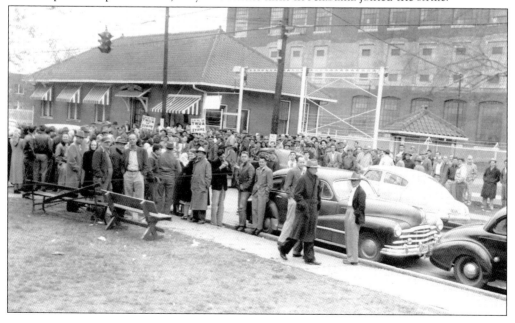

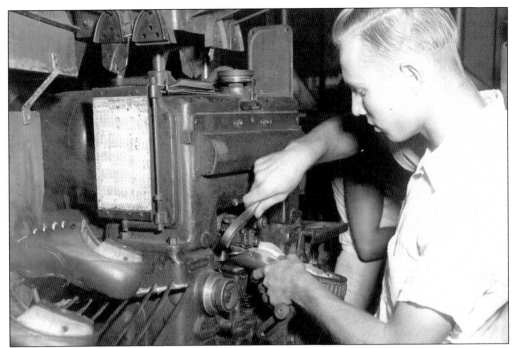

The Genesco Inc. Shoe Factory began production as the General Shoe Factory in the Lowe Mill building in 1946. It employed 100 workers, many of whom were returning World War II soldiers. The company received a $1 million contract from the US Army to make 180,000 pairs of field shoes. Genesco closed in 1978, leaving 700 full-time workers looking for new jobs.

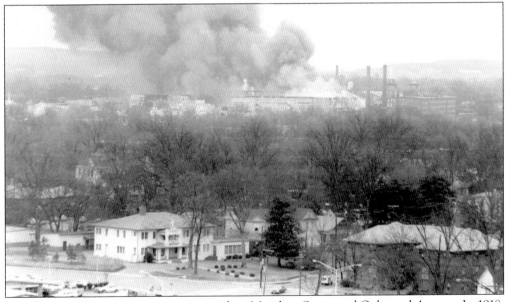

In 1900, a small spinning company opened on Meridian Street and Oakwood Avenue. In 1918, when it was known as Abingdon Mills, William Lincoln Barrell of Lowell, Massachusetts, purchased the property, making it into one of Huntsville's largest mills before it closed in 1957. The building was sold and renamed the Huntsville Industrial Center (HIC). The oldest portion of the building burned on February 19, 1980.

Six

THE GOOD AND BAD OF BECOMING HUNTSVILLE

Huntsville, like any other town, has had its highs and lows. It has survived many tragedies, including fires, floods, and other natural disasters. During the Civil War, Union troops moved in and occupied the town, creating turmoil between the federal government and Huntsvillians, and many homes and buildings were burned. After the Civil War, African Americans built schools and joined the local political arena. During the Spanish-American War, the people once again came together to join in a combined effort. Public and private schools were built to educate Huntsville's citizens. Cotton and textile mills brought prosperity to Huntsville.

The Depression brought with it hard times for farmers, mill workers, and businessmen in the city, and the crime rate increased. Mill workers went on strike and labor unions were formed. World War II brought many changes to Huntsville, including the addition of munitions manufacturing to Redstone Arsenal, boosting Huntsville's economy. When World War II ended, the munitions plants were shut down and the residents feared another economic depression. Shortly after, however, a team of German rocket scientists and engineers moved to Huntsville and quickly transformed the city into what is now known as Rocket City, USA.

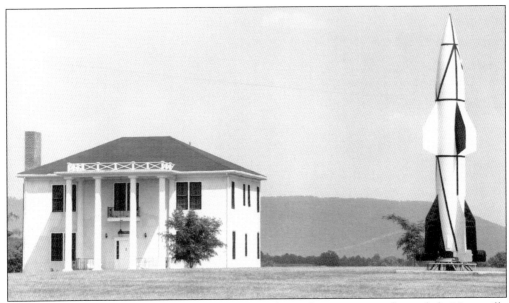

Redstone Arsenal became an important military facility and a new source of growth for Huntsville during World War II. Although the federal government removed many family farms and homes to make room for the new post, the arsenal immediately created 550 new jobs in the Huntsville area. Redstone Arsenal continues to stimulate growth in northern Alabama. This photograph symbolizes the blending of Huntsville's past and future.

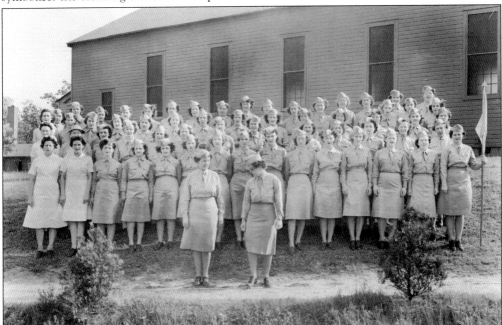

In December 1943, the *Huntsville Times* reported that the first members of the Women's Army Corps (WAC) had arrived in the city. During World War II, more than 150,000 women served in the military as something other than a nurse. Applicants were required to be between 21 and 45 years old, have no dependents, and weigh more than 100 pounds. This photograph was taken on May 6, 1944.

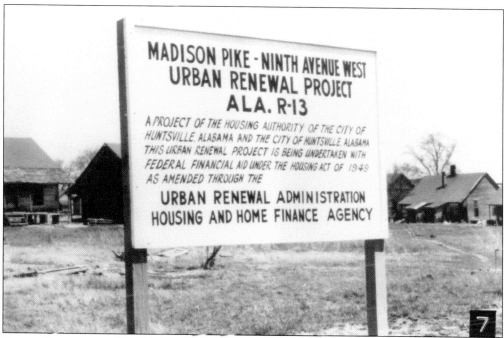

Responding to a post World War II housing shortage, Pres. Harry S. Truman signed the American Housing Act of 1949 and ushered in an urban renewal movement that destroyed many of Huntsville's beautiful Victorian homes and irreplaceable historical landmarks. It became easy for lawmakers to wipe away old buildings in the name of progress, and in Jim Crow Alabama, it was not surprising that St. Bartley Primitive Baptist Church (below), the oldest black church in Alabama, established by slaves, was destroyed. The church was originally organized in 1820 around a burial site for slaves that came to be known as Old Georgia Graveyard. A new church was eventually built and the first worship service at the new location was in 1965.

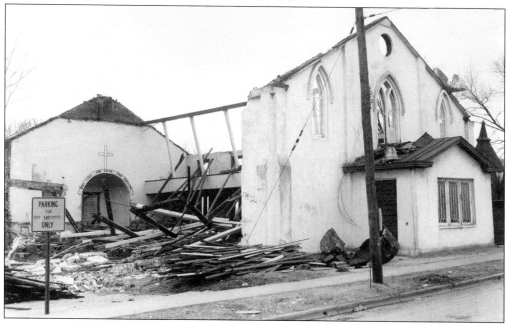

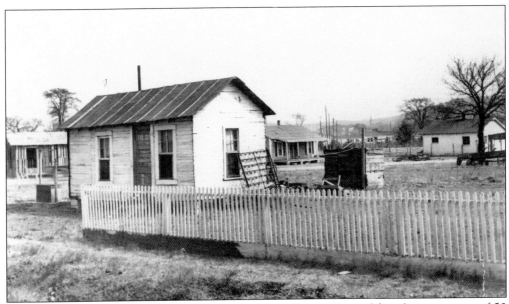

Sometimes referred to as Dixie Village or Brogtown, Booger Town (above) was an area of 50 shanty homes near downtown Huntsville. The city first tried to clean up the area in 1947. Later, city officials cleared the area to make way for low-income housing and to rid West Huntsville of its most recognizable slum. The burning of Booger Town (below) began a controversial period in the city's history, marked by urban renewal and population removal. Many of these families had already lost their land after the government moved them from the area that is now Redstone Arsenal. It is important to remember that "progress" often comes at a price for those seen as an obstruction or a blemish.

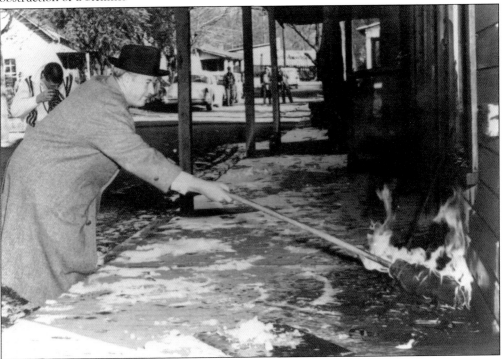

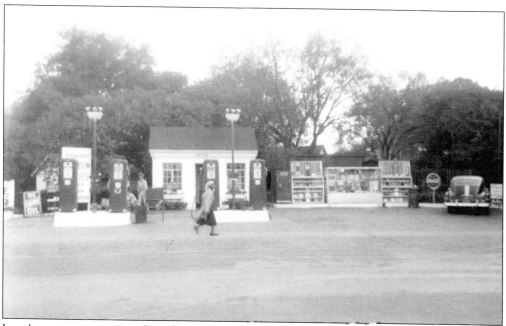

Local preservationists conducted a photographic survey of Huntsville's gas stations in the early 1950s. Many of these photographs are now housed in the Huntsville–Madison County Public Library and are accessible on Alabama Mosaic. The library's digital archives have an online exhibit called *Full Service: The Glory Days of Huntsville Gas Stations*. As seen above, Winn Spur Oil on Clinton Street had a large outdoor display of dishes that could be earned through customer loyalty. Bill Thrower's gas station on Meridian Street (below) featured beautiful wooden detailing. The sign on the front window announces that the station was closed on Sundays. Both photographs were taken in 1956.

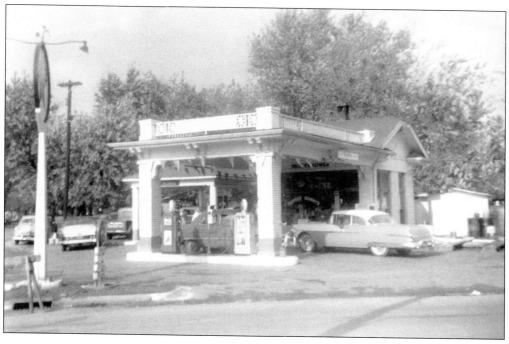

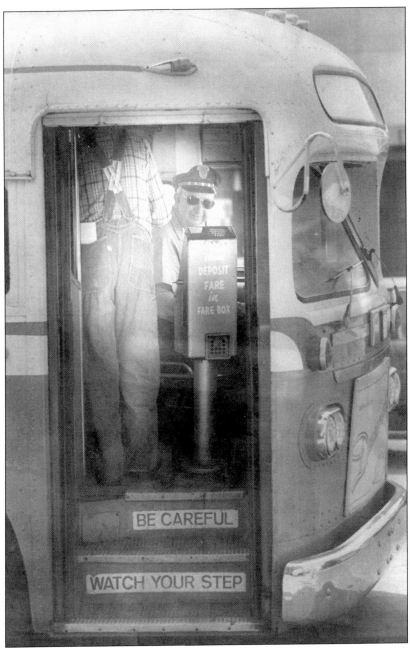

BE CAREFUL

WATCH YOUR STEP

Public transportation and mass transit have been a common theme for generations of residents. The *Huntsville Daily Times* reported the end of the electric streetcar on February 22, 1931, with a headline that read, "Buses to Traverse City Over Regular Routes, Street Cars Have Run Thirty Years." Later, in 1976, the *Huntsville Times* reported the end of public buses in Huntsville. This photograph, dated June 24, 1976, was taken in the final stages of the old public bus system. James W. Carter welcomed his passengers with a courteous "Welcome aboard." In 1977, Huntsville Transit had three routes, one to Parkway City Mall and two from the downtown area that catered to domestic workers. Carter is buried with his wife, Sina, in Maple Hill Cemetery. He died on February 2, 1985, five years before buses returned with the city-operated Huntsville Shuttle Bus.

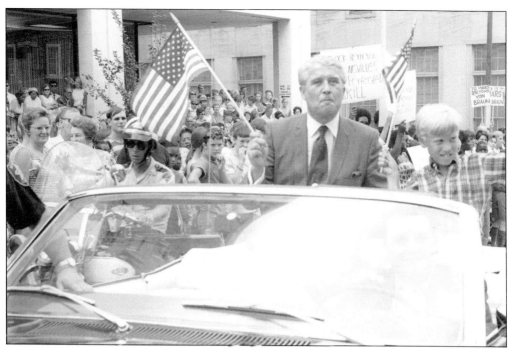

On July 24, 1969, Dr. Wernher von Braun and his son Peter wave to excited crowds in Huntsville after Apollo 11 successfully splashed down. Von Braun, a German scientist who moved to Huntsville after World War II, became a hero in the minds of many city residents. Note the several protesters in the crowd holding signs that highlight frustration over urban renewal projects and unfair racial laws.

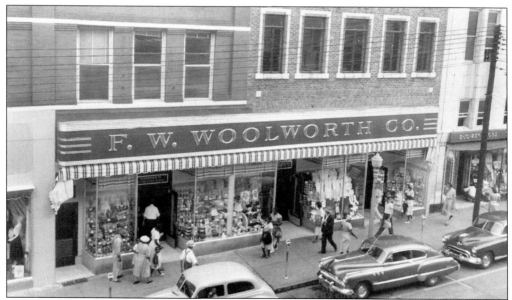

Huntsville had its share of civil disobedience, with sit-ins and protests occurring during the Civil Rights era. The Woolworth's at Heart of Huntsville Mall, W.T. Grant's restaurant, Walgreens, and Sear's coffee shop were among the businesses where demonstrations took place. This is a view of a demonstration at the Woolworth's on Washington Street.

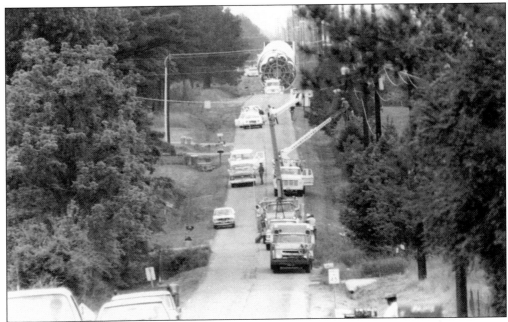

Crews moving the 224-foot Saturn 1B rocket along local roads to the Alabama welcome center made national news on May 10, 1979. This rocket became one of the most identifiable landmarks for a city growing around the space program and missile defense. Thousands of drivers pass the United States Space and Rocket Center and this rocket on a daily basis.

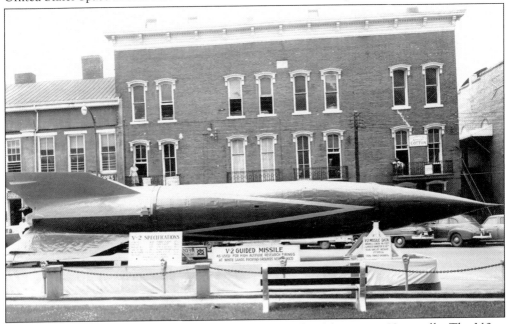

A V-2 missile stands in front of buildings on the west side of downtown Huntsville. The V-2, a rocket developed by many of Huntsville's German scientists, was used to attack Allied soldiers and civilians during World War II. After the war, it served as a prototype for the US rocket program. The building behind the rocket was torn down in 1966 and replaced with benches and stairs leading down to Big Spring Park.

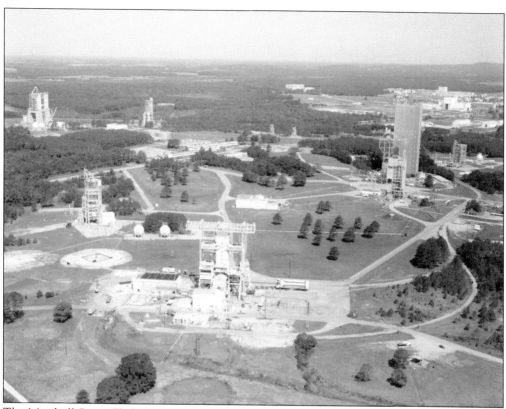

The Marshall Space Flight Center (MSFC) and the NASA test stand facility are seen above in 1977. On January 22, 1986, the MSFC's office of history announced that four MSFC facilities were deemed National Historic Landmarks. Today, those four facilities—the Propulsion and Structural Test Facility, the Saturn V Dynamic Test Stand, the Neutral Buoyancy Simulator, and the Saturn V—serve as reminders of NASA's imprint on Huntsville's past. Below, Thiokol workers load Maverick Motors for transport in September 1975. The Thiokol Chemical Company was established in 1929, first producing a synthetic rubber before becoming famous for developing a stabilizer in solid-fuel rockets.

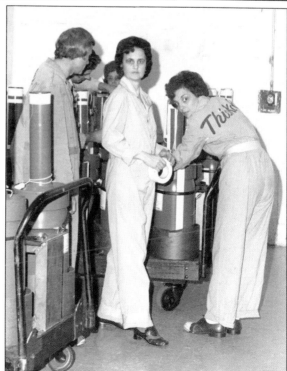

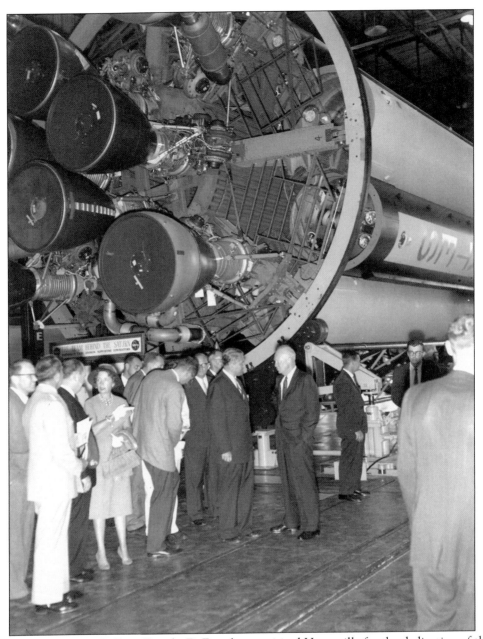

On September 8, 1960, Pres. Dwight D. Eisenhower visited Huntsville for the dedication of the Marshall Space Flight Center. He is seen here in the center speaking with Wernher von Braun in front of a Saturn rocket. The sign reads, "The Team Behind the Saturn." President Eisenhower's visit was big news for the citizens of Huntsville, and the *Huntsville Times*'s coverage of his visit included a pictorial history that featured key moments such as the dedication of a red granite bust of Gen. George C. Marshall. The *Times* reported that Eisenhower "took a left-handed swing at the Soviets," and credited the country's success to "hard work, toughness of spirit and self-reliant enterprise, and not to soulless barren technology nor of a grasping state imperialism." When Eisenhower toured the facilities, he reportedly looked up at the giant Saturn and said, "It would take quite an engineering work to hold this thing together."

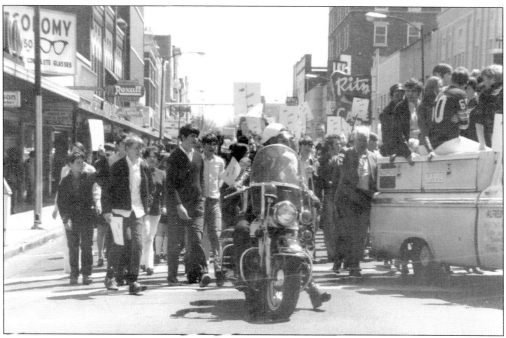

On March 31, 1971, local protestors took to the streets of downtown Huntsville to show their support for Lt. William Calley after he was accused of leading the My Lai massacre during the Vietnam War in March 1968. Although many Americans protested the country's involvement in the Vietnam War, Huntsville residents in these two photographs show their support for Lieutenant Calley, arguing that he had become a scapegoat for federal investigators looking to shift the blame away from those who had ordered the killing of women and children. In 2009, Calley apologized for his role in the massacre.

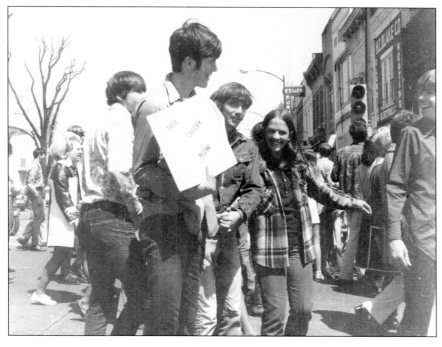

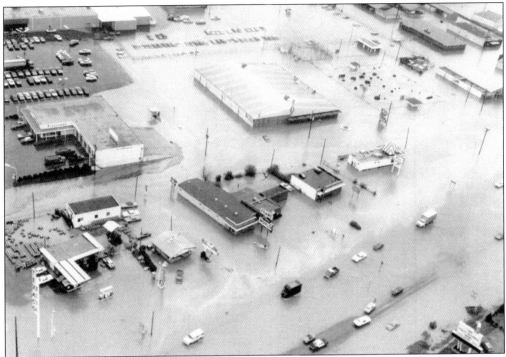

On March 16, 1973, Huntsville experienced the largest flash flood in its recorded history. This photograph shows the high waters at the intersection of Leeman Ferry Road and Bob Wallace Avenue. Many of the businesses in this photograph, including Firestone, Frame World, Kentucky Fried Chicken, and the bowling alley, are still in their same locations.

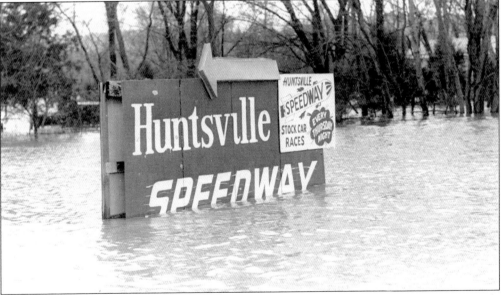

The 1973 flood reached as far as the Huntsville Speedway, off Hobbs Island Road. The fittingly named A.E. Speed founded the speedway in 1959. Many Southern cities and towns hosted local racecar drivers who wanted to show off their vehicles and thrill race fans. Many early racers started doing it as moonshiners, fleeing the police in hopped-up cars during Prohibition.

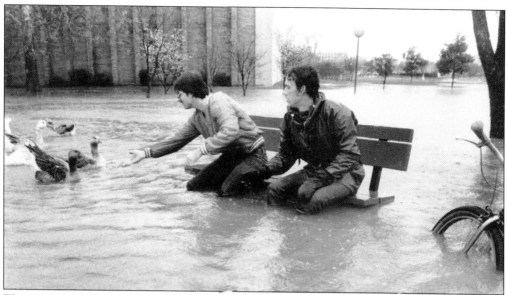

The citizens of Huntsville, the United States Missile Command, and the Army donated boats to the rescue effort following the 1973 flood. There were no reports of any deaths in Huntsville despite extensive property damage. The two men above ventured into the flooded area of Big Spring Park on bicycles and were photographed feeding ducks. Some city officials called it a 100-year flood after the *Huntsville Times* reported six inches of torrential downpour over a period of only a few hours. Heavy rains caused Big Spring to flood (below), and water covered the parkway from Governor's Drive to Drake Avenue.

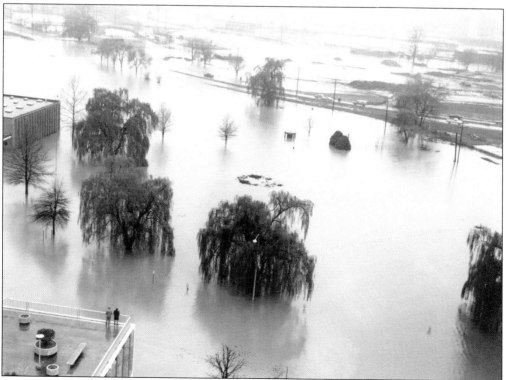

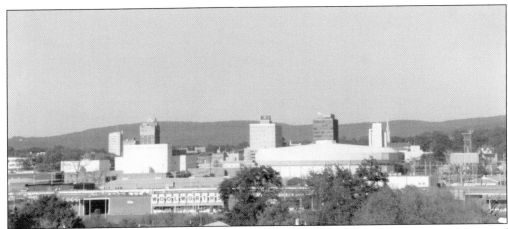

In the 1970s, the rounded dome of the $11 million Von Braun Civic Center became part of Huntsville's skyline. The unobstructed views of Monte Sano had given way to a modern city and many buildings, such as the magnificent Russell Erskine Hotel (second tall building from the left), and the Madison County Courthouse (above the center of the dome).

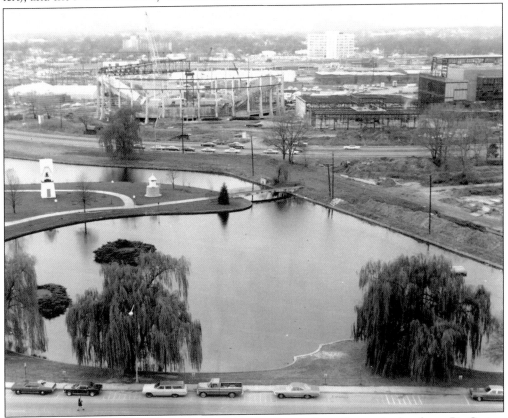

This photograph shows the construction of the Von Braun Civic Center. It also shows Big Spring Park before the planting of Japanese cherry trees and the construction of the Red Bridge and a nearby parking garage. On July 9, 1973, a dedication ceremony in Big Spring International Park was held to commemorate gifts from around the world such as the light beacon, fog bell, and tower in the center of the park.

Seven

THE ODDS AND ENDS
OF LIFE IN HUNTSVILLE

As World War II came to an end, munitions manufacturers in Huntsville knew their jobs would end. Many feared the worst, as Alabama, a low-tech state, did not have much to offer high-tech companies. Thankfully, the economic recession after the war did not last long. By 1950, a team of rocket scientists and their families had moved to Huntsville. The city was selected based on its location and landscape. German and American rocket scientists and engineers began working on what became the space program. In doing so, they made Huntsville the bustling city it is now. However, life in Huntsville continued to be a diverse mixture of odds and ends. These photographs capture city residents going about their daily lives and participating in special events.

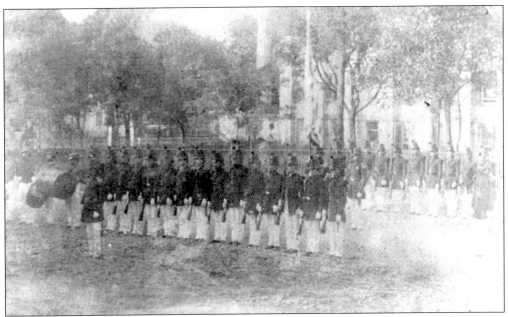

The Civil War brought challenging times and circumstances for city residents. Union lieutenant William Lytle recalled, "Alas it is no Happy Valley now. The desolating footstep of the war has gone over it and it will tell with pallid lips in years to come the bloody history of this accursed rebellion." In April 1862, Union troops occupied the city, creating anxiety for many residents who supported the Confederate States of America, and joy for local Unionists who continued to support the Union despite living in the Deep South. The Madison Rifles (above), organized as a home guard and social club in 1855, began to drill and train for war. The unit left Huntsville on March 26, 1861, joining the 1st Alabama Infantry Regiment. The photograph below shows the 84th Illinois Infantry Regiment, which set up camp around Courthouse Square.

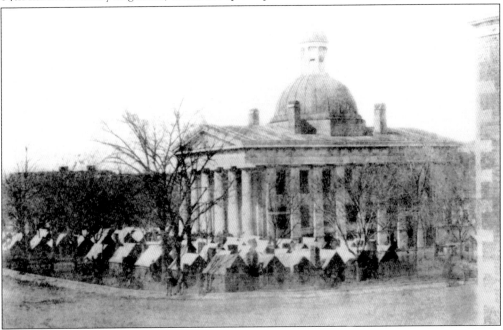

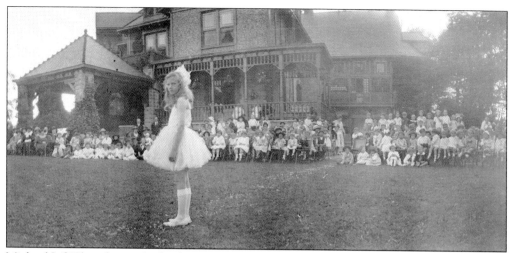

Michael J. O'Shaughnessy built what is known as the Kildare Home in 1886. It eventually became the seasonal residence of Virginia McCormick, the daughter of Cyrus H. McCormick, the inventor of the mechanical reaper. With the help of her companion, Grace Walker, McCormick became a generous local philanthropist. The Kildare Home is seen here during an Easter egg hunt.

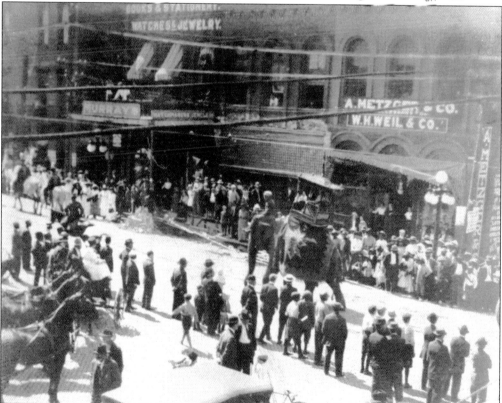

The jungle came to Huntsville when elephants from the Ringling Brothers Circus marched through downtown in 1909. Eager residents hoped to catch a glimpse of the hundreds of exotic animals that arrived on a train with 85 railroad cars. The circus continues to stop in Huntsville, and modern residents still get excited when animals parade through the city.

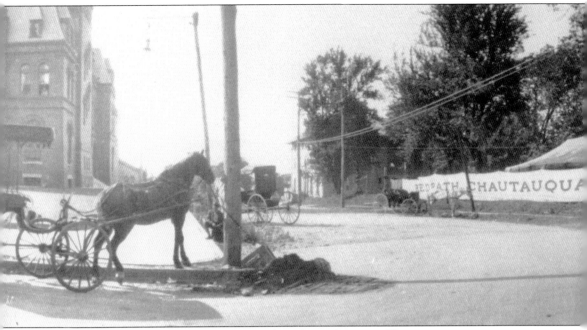

The Redpath Chautauqua, one of a number of traveling tent Chautauquas, was an important social event in Huntsville. Chautauquas strove to educate and entertain through a series of popular lectures along with group discussions and performances. People from around the area would travel to Huntsville to participate, adding additional revenue to city coffers. In addition to the tent, the old Huntsville post office can be seen on the left. On Greene Street between

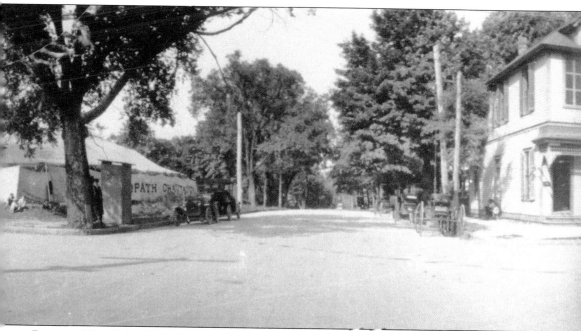

Eustis and Randolph Streets, the post office was razed to make room for a parking lot in 1954. Suburban development after World War II de-emphasized the importance of downtown buildings. By the early 1970s, good roads, new neighborhoods, and urban sprawl had stifled Huntsville's downtown development.

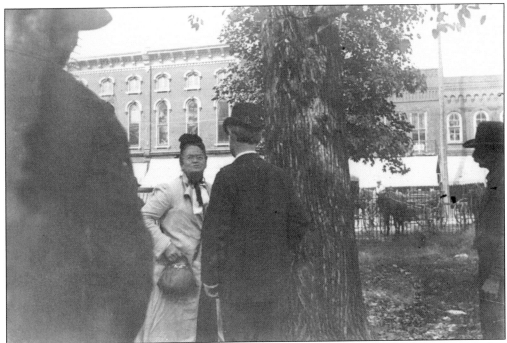

Carrie Nation, a militant temperance leader, came to Huntsville to wage war against alcohol in 1902. It was reported that while she held a Bible in one hand and spoke about her raids on saloons, she also carried her ever-present hatchet. After her speech, she visited several local saloons, where she gave the proprietors scorching lectures on the evils of drink.

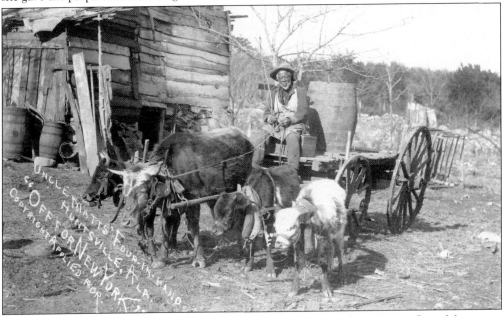

"Uncle Matt" was a colorful local character who lived with his wife on Monte Sano Mountain. After the Spanish-American War, Uncle Matt drove this team of oxen all the way to New York City and led the victory parade down Fifth Avenue. The original caption to this photograph reads, "Uncle Matt's Roamin' Chariot."

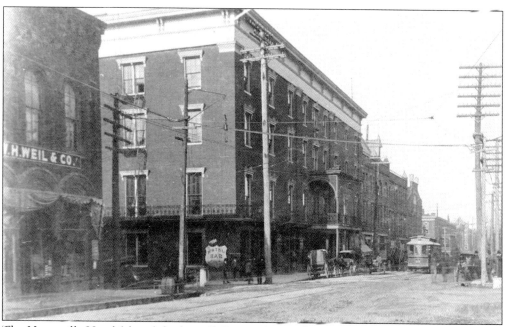

The Huntsville Hotel (above), built in 1858, was Huntsville's premier spot for visitors, including Gen. George Custer, who stayed there in 1873. James O'Shaughnessy purchased the hotel in 1887 and began to modernize it, adding an annex with 65 rooms. Soon after, the "mosquito free" hotel advertised modern conveniences such as gas lamps, elevators, a steam laundry, a fully equipped bar, and a billiards area. The hotel hosted many balls and parties and served as the meeting place for the Huntsville Business College and the North Alabama Improvement Company, a group largely responsible for Huntsville's industrial boom. In 1896, Huntsville mayor W.T. Hutchens placed the very first long-distance call from Huntsville, after which a grand celebration ensued. Fire eventually destroyed the grand hotel as locals watched helplessly.

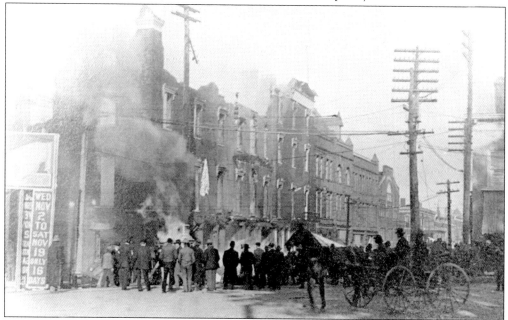

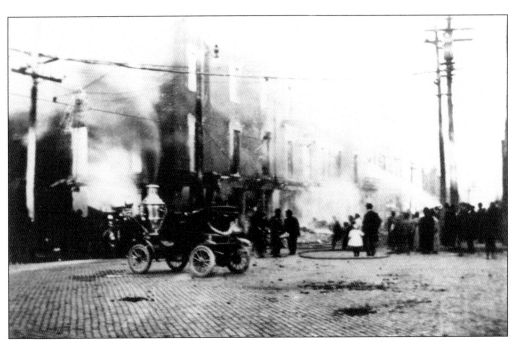

City residents watched with great sorrow as fire destroyed the Huntsville Hotel on November 4, 1910. Newspapers reported that bad wiring caused the fire. A year later, another great fire struck, this time in the early morning hours of November 5, 1911, and destroyed an entire city block of Jefferson Street between Clinton and Spring Streets. The second fire destroyed the remnants of the hotel as well as multiple businesses and the Huntsville Opera House. Adjusters estimated that the blaze destroyed $250,000 worth of property. Most American cities experienced regular fires around that time, which wiped out large portions of historic districts. These burned-out sections of towns were then redeveloped with more modern architectural styles and building materials.

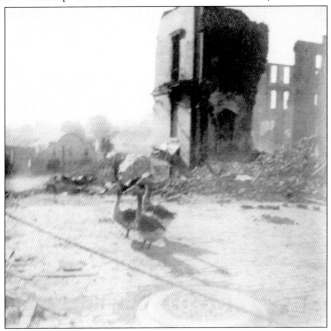

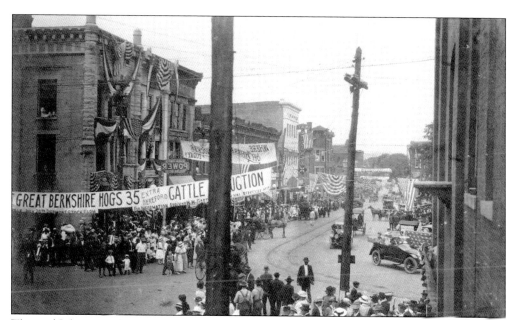

The mid-July scene above on the east side of Courthouse Square features signs and banners advertising an auction to be held for Great Berkshire hogs and cattle near the Schiffman Building. Note the number of men and women wearing hats and long-sleeved clothing on this hot Alabama day.

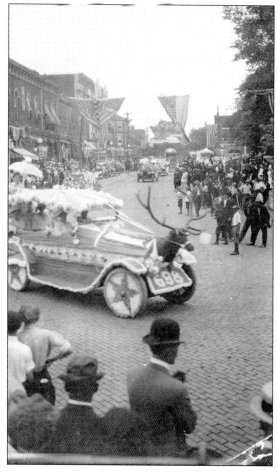

Elks Lodge No. 698 won first prize for this float in the 1915 Fourth of July parade. Mamie S. Mays, the driver, peers out of the front window of the decorated car. The city's Elks Lodge was chartered by 35 members in 1901, but closed in 1917. In 1942, Elks Lodge No. 1648 reemerged in the city and continues to function today in its lodge off of Franklin Street.

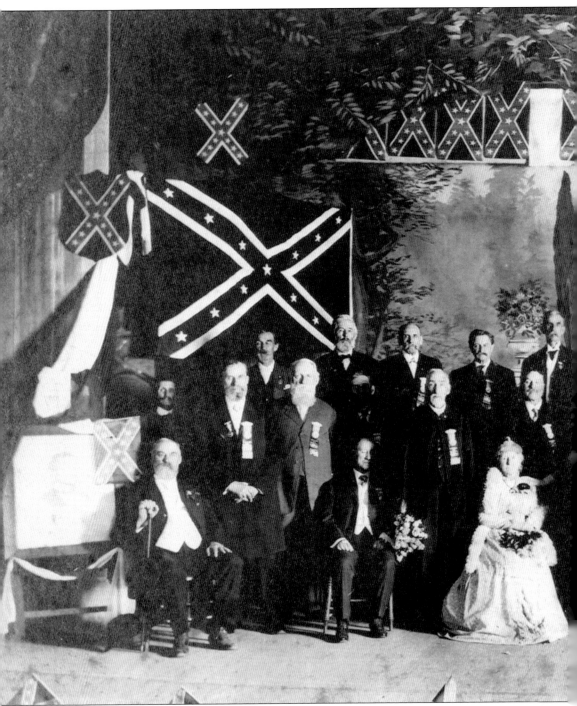

This photograph shows the return of a Confederate battle flag to Alabama. A member of the 4th Ohio Volunteer Cavalry had captured the flag during the Battle of Selma on April 2, 1865. Mrs. Charles G. Brown, the president of the United Daughters of the Confederacy (UDC), discovered the flag in the Ohio Statehouse Relic Room. Brown requested that Ohio governor Judson Harmon return the flag to Alabama. He agreed and returned the flag during Alabama's United Daughters

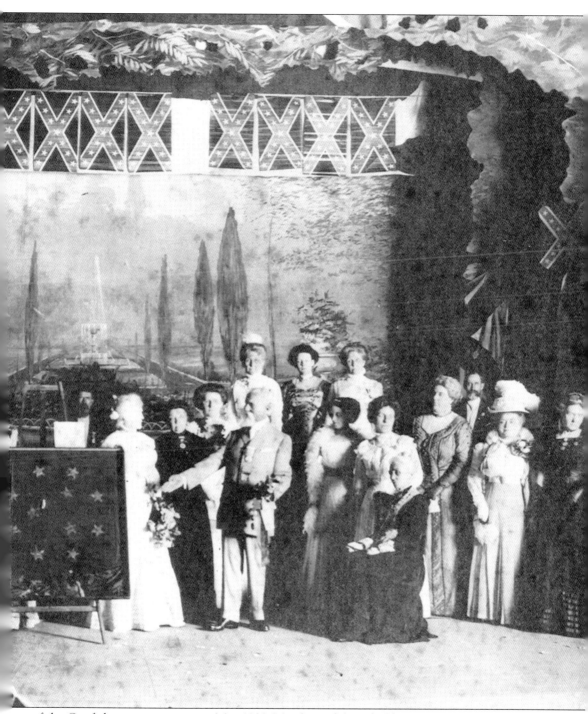

of the Confederacy convention in May 1909. Members of the 4th Ohio Regiment returned the flag as a symbol of national unity. Seated from left to right are Huntsville mayor T.W. Smith, James Quinton (4th Ohio Regiment), Virginia Clay (Clopton UDC), and Helen Plaine. (Courtesy of the Alabama Department of Archives and History.)

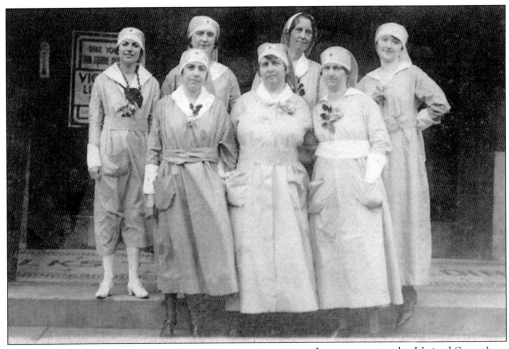

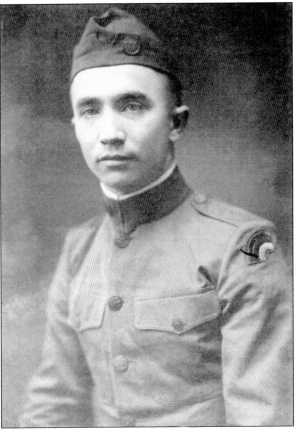

In response to the United States's entrance into World War I, the American Red Cross formed a chapter in northern Alabama. Red Cross chapters across America were dedicated to raising both funds and awareness for the war effort. The seven women above wear the attire typical of nurses at the time. The war presented a unique opportunity for women to expand their roles in American society. In Huntsville, 4,000 men volunteered to fight. One of them was Lee Harless, who wears the Rainbow Division patch proudly on his shoulder in the portrait at left. In August 1917, the soldiers of the Alabama National Guard became part of the 42nd Rainbow Division.

Dr. Carl August Grote Sr., Alabama's first full-time county health officer, traveled to Huntsville after an outbreak of typhoid fever in 1915. He discovered that Big Spring, downtown Huntsville's main water supply, carried the bacterial disease responsible for the illness spreading across the city. In 1918, he moved to Huntsville to help with the Spanish flu epidemic.

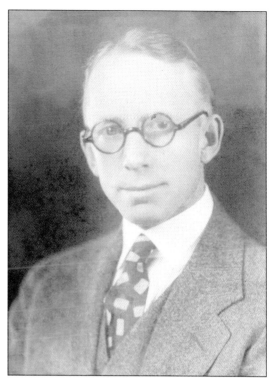

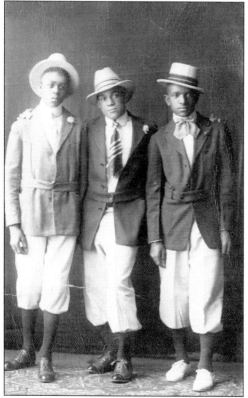

Posing for a photograph in the early 1900s meant dressing up and making a day of it. These three young city residents posed in their best ties, knickerbockers, and boutonnieres. Their hats were typical for fashionable men, who could pick between fedoras, homburgs, and trilby hats, or a simple straw boater on a hot summer day.

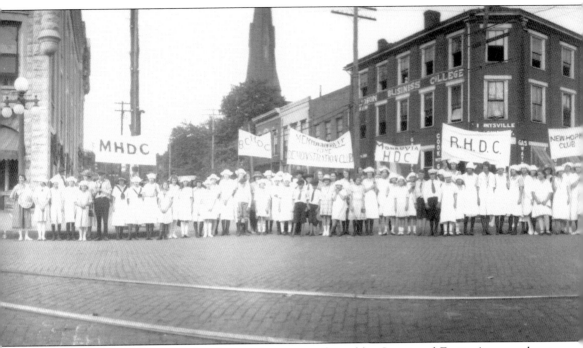

This panoramic photograph, taken at the corner of Franklin Street and Eustis Avenue, shows the corner of the Schiffman Building, Harrison Brothers Hardware (right), and the steeple of the Church of Nativity (left background). These women had gathered for a meeting of the local Home Demonstration Club, an extension of the federal government's rural improvement program. The

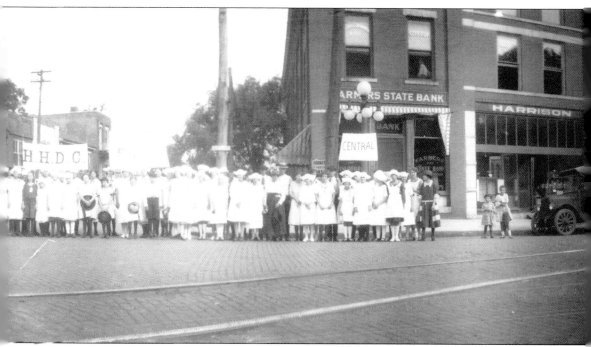

organization's promotional literature noted that the club "provided training not only in nutrition, hygiene, and child-rearing techniques but also in craft skills useful to home-making and developing home industries." Alabama home-demonstration specialist Isadora Williams helped promote these cottage industries, which included products like rag rugs and baskets.

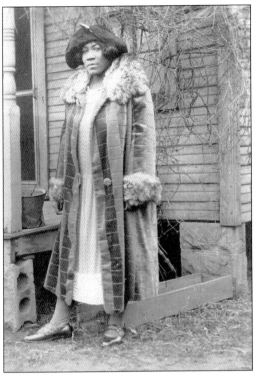

A city resident poses for a photograph in front of a wood-frame house with its porch propped up by a cinder block. This photograph was most likely taken by a traveling photographer sometime in the winter. This coat, with its full fur collar and cuffs, is a fine example of the style in the 1920s and 1930s.

On August 15, 1945, joyful residents gathered in Big Spring Park to listen to D.C. Monroe's big band and celebrate the end of World War II. Dan Castello Monroe came to Huntsville in 1888 to direct the Monte Sano Hotel orchestra. Later, he opened Huntsville's first music store as well as the Monroe Printing Company. He died on October 12, 1957.

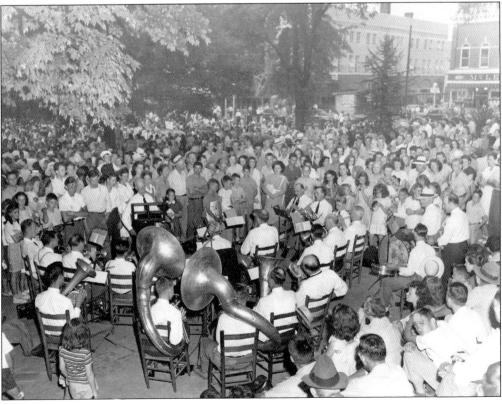

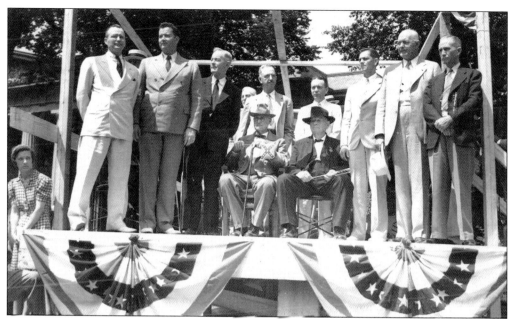

Attendees at the 1939 Monte Sano Celebration celebrate the last two living Confederate veterans in Madison County. John A. Steger, with the cane, served in Company G of General Roddy's 4th Alabama Cavalry. Next to him in the black hat is W.T. "Bill" Bennett, who fought with Company C of the 25th Alabama Cavalry.

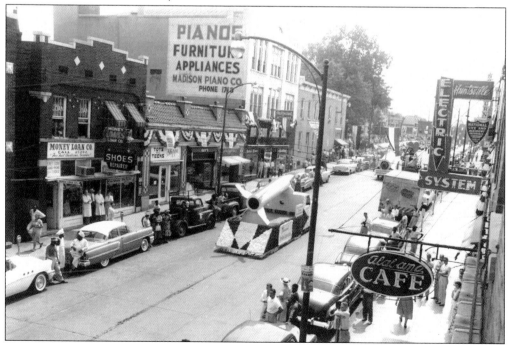

By the 1950s, celebrations and parades often contained floats with rockets and various space-age technologies, showing the influence of Redstone Arsenal. This street scene mixes rocketry with traditional businesses such as the Alabama Café. There are also signs for Money Loan Co., Goodyear Shoe Shop, and Huntsville Electric System.

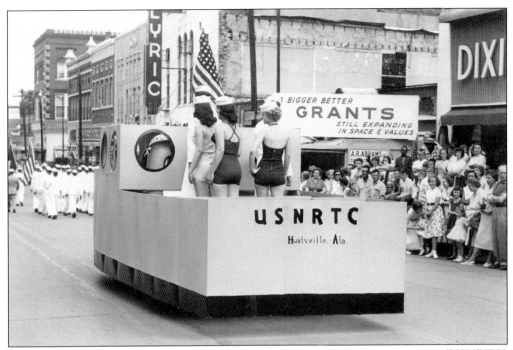

This 1955 parade scene shows the United States Naval Reserve Training Center (USNRTC) float in front of the Lyric Theater on Washington Street. Dunnavant's Department Store is on the corner in the background. Note the bathing suit styles of the 1950s.

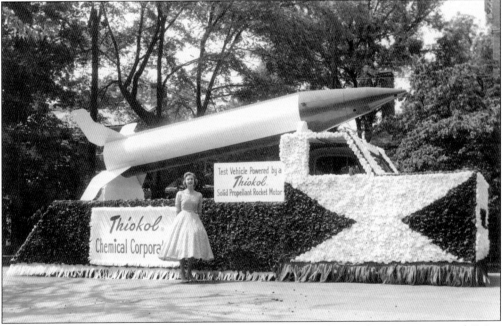

Thiokol's float for the 1955 sesquicentennial parade is seen here. The woman, named "Miss Wooley Booger" was the group sweetheart for the Thiokol Wooley Booger group in the Brothers of the Brush sesquicentennial organization. Thiokol Chemical Corporation was one of the first government contractors at Redstone Arsenal.

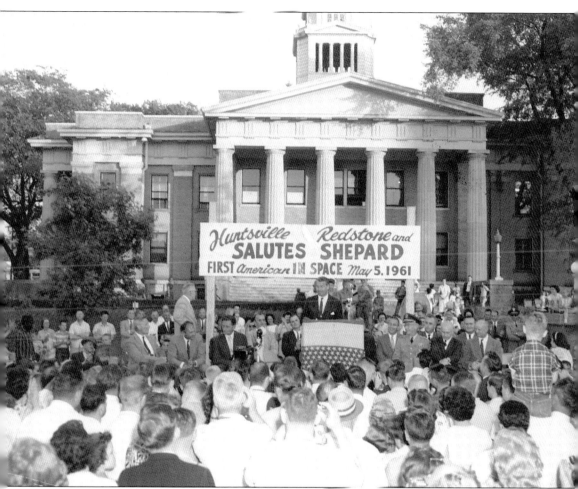

Wernher von Braun flew in from Cape Canaveral to commemorate Comdr. Alan B. Shepard, the first American to ride a rocket into space. Commander Shepard achieved this goal on a Redstone rocket on May 5, 1961. The original caption on the back of this photograph states, "115 mile ride at a speed of 5,100 miles per hour."

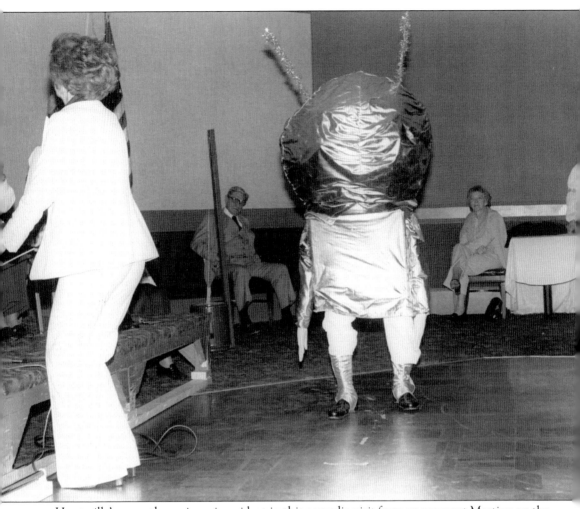

Huntsville's space theme is again evident in this comedic visit from an apparent Martian on the dance floor at the Huntsville Hilton Veteran's Day celebration on November 11, 1979. The next day, the mood of downtown Huntsville was less jovial, as local university students held a rally for the American hostages held in Iran.

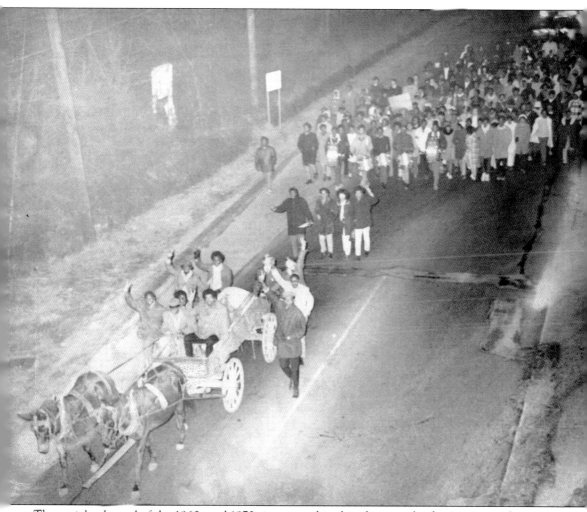

The social upheaval of the 1960s and 1970s is captured in this photograph of university students marching in Huntsville. In December 1969, students at Alabama A&M and the University of Alabama in Huntsville organized a large rally and march against America's involvement in the Vietnam War.

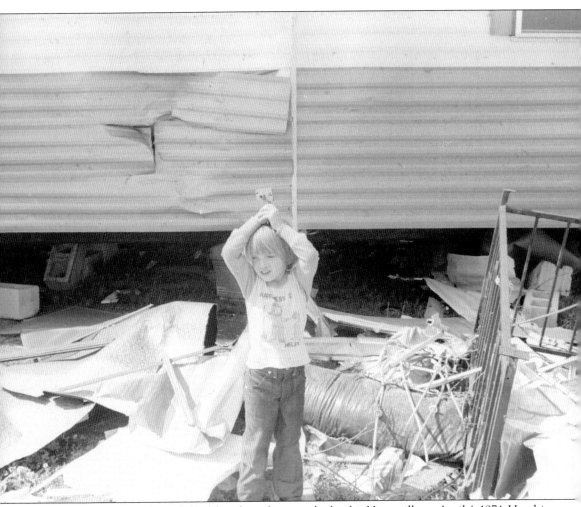

This little girl stands amid the debris from the tornado that hit Huntsville on April 4, 1974. Her shirt has a person holding a broom and dustpan and reads, "Happiness is Help." It was reported in the *Huntsville Times* that several people died during the storms and more than 200 were injured.

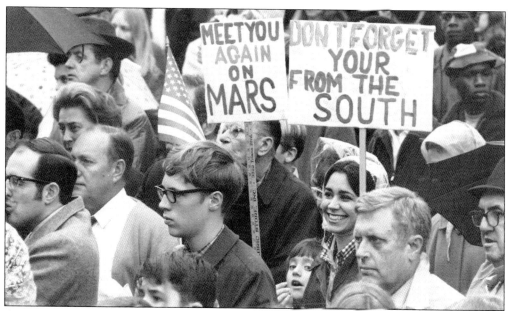

On February 3, 1970, Dr. Wernher von Braun made public his plans to leave Huntsville. Festivities were arranged to commemorate his departure. A parade was held downtown on the public square, and February 24, 1970, was celebrated as Wernher von Braun Day. It was also announced that Huntsville's new civic center, estimated to cost $10 million, would be named in his honor. Eberhard Rees became the next director of the Marshall Space Flight Center. Huntsville residents said goodbye to Von Braun with signs saying "Meet You Again on Mars" (above) and "Auf Wiedersehen" (below). Although it seemed that the city's future would be hurt by his loss, Huntsville, as it had since the early 1800s, reinvented itself once again. Today, it is home to thousands of new residents looking for new challenges in the 21st century.

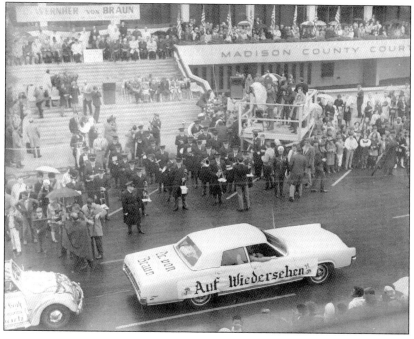

DISCOVER THOUSANDS OF LOCAL HISTORY BOOKS FEATURING MILLIONS OF VINTAGE IMAGES

Arcadia Publishing, the leading local history publisher in the United States, is committed to making history accessible and meaningful through publishing books that celebrate and preserve the heritage of America's people and places.

Find more books like this at
www.arcadiapublishing.com

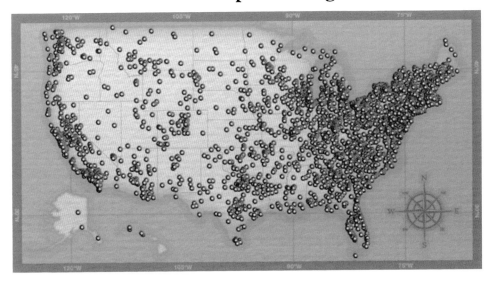

Search for your hometown history, your old stomping grounds, and even your favorite sports team.

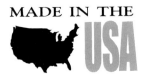